The Amazing Animal Activity Book

Dozens of Creative Hands-On Projects That Teach Across the Curriculum

by Robin Bernard

SCHOLASTIC
PROFESSIONAL BOOKS

New York ▪ Toronto ▪ London ▪ Auckland ▪ Sydney

Dedication

For Roberta and Barbara, sisters who are like friends; and for Rita, Bobbi, and Nancy — friends who are like sisters.

Acknowledgements

My thanks to Ingrid Blinken for her fine editorial touch. It was a pleasure writing this book, and she made it even more so. And my gratitude also to Dr. B. Grzimek, founder of the Serengeti Research Institute, for inviting me to share the wonders of African wildlife so long ago.

Interior design by Jaime Lucero and Robert Dominguez for Grafica, Inc.
Interior illustrations by Robin Bernard, Delana Betolli and Carmen Sorvillo
Cover design by Jaime Lucero
Cover photography by Donnelly Marks

ISBN 0-590-96404-6

Table of Contents

INTRODUCTION 4
POEM: A CELEBRATION 6

Chapter 1: Mammals
BACKGROUND INFORMATION 7
STUDENT ACTIVITIES 8

Chapter 2: Reptiles

BACKGROUND INFORMATION 27
STUDENT ACTIVITIES 28

Chapter 3: Amphibians
BACKGROUND INFORMATION 43
STUDENT ACTIVITIES 44

Chapter 4: Fish

BACKGROUND INFORMATION 59
STUDENT ACTIVITIES 60

Chapter 5: Birds
BACKGROUND INFORMATION 77
STUDENT ACTIVITIES 78

Chapter 6:
The Animal Kingdom

BACKGROUND INFORMATION 95
STUDENT ACTIVITIES 97

The Amazing Animal Activity Book

WELCOME TO THE WORLD OF WILDLIFE!

It's hard to think of anything that fascinates children as much as animals do—or anything that inspires as many questions! You'll probably be bombarded with them, so each section of this book begins with supportive background information for you. Your students may ask do all birds fly? Are reptiles and amphibians the same thing? Do all mammals have fur? They'll find the answers to many of their questions on the **All About** . . . reference page at the beginning of each activity section. They'll make a lot of other wildlife discoveries as they become involved in fun activities designed to encourage their scientific curiosity as well as their creativity.

Here are a few suggestions to help you get the most out of this book.

1 PICK AND CHOOSE

Although leading your students on a page-by-page safari might be fun, you may want to use the activities as they relate to a specific part of your curriculum. For instance, if you are studying oceans, you can find activities about fish, sea-mammals, and penguins; if you are studying climate, you might select the activity on hibernation. In addition, you can easily adapt, alter, and develop spin-off projects that are best suited to your students' abilities and interests.

2 FIND OUT WHAT YOUR STUDENTS REALLY WANT TO KNOW

The activities are intended as a foundation, a way for children to learn about characteristics that define different animal groups. The order in which they're used isn't very important, but if you find out what really intrigues the children, the activities will be especially effective tools. Your students might be more interested in how camouflage works than in how different animals got their names. They may be less interested in why some animals are nocturnal than in how those animals manage to find food in the dark. Since children are delighted by surprises, they'll enjoy discovering some birds that don't fly, and a mammal that does!

3 TRADE BOOKS CAN ENRICH WILDLIFE TOPICS

Try to assemble a classroom library of fiction and nonfiction animal books, appropriate for all reading levels (see **Book Breaks** at the end of each chapter for suggestions). Be sure to set aside some quiet time for kids to explore the books and make more wonderful discoveries. And since they love having stories read to them, don't forget to include the read-alouds.

4 CELEBRATE AS YOU GO

Set up a bulletin board to celebrate what the children have learned about the animal kingdom. Use it to display their drawings, puppets, and other projects. Hang their mobiles. Invite them to paint pictures of their favorite animals, and display them prominently on the walls.

NOTE: While insects are not discussed in great detail in this book, they are an integral part of the animal kingdom. To help your students learn more about these champions of survival, share the following trade books with them:

From Caterpillar to Butterfly by Deborah Heiligman (HarperTrophy, 1996)

Worldwise Insects & Spiders by Penny Clarke (Franklin Watts, 1995)

Creepy Crawlies by Cathy Kilpatrick (Usborne First Nature, 1990)

In order to make the activities more meaningful, be sure to spend some time discussing the following definitions:

CARNIVORE—a meat eater

HERBIVORE—a plant eater

OMNIVORE—a meat and plant eater

NOCTURNAL—active at night

HIBERNATION—a deep winter "sleep"

MIGRATION—a seasonal trip to a specific place

CAMOUFLAGE—colors and patterns that blend with the surroundings

You might even ask students to brainstorm examples of animals that fit into these categories.

A Celebration

On our whirling, twirling planet
there are creatures everywhere
on the land and in the oceans,
riding, gliding through the air.
From bees that buzz on flowers
to whales singing their own songs,
we're all pieces of a puzzle—
each connects and each belongs.
Maybe there are other creatures
in some distant galaxy,
but let's celebrate
all those who share
green Earth
with you. . .
and me!

—Bobbi Katz

Distribute a copy of the poem to each student. You may want to read the poem to the class first and then have them read it together. Invite students to color the animals and add some of their own.

CHAPTER 1

Big Brains
Mammals

BACKGROUND INFORMATION

There are far fewer kinds of mammals than there are fish or birds, but even with less than 5,000 species, they still present an enormous variety of sizes and shapes—from a one and half inch shrew, to a whale a hundred feet in length! The characteristics that distinguish mammals from other endothermic (warm-blooded), air-breathing vertebrates are their large brains, production of milk for the young, and to varying degrees—hair. We think of mammals as "furry," but some, like dolphins and whales, have only a few hairs on their snouts which fall out shortly after birth. As a rule, mammals give birth to live young—but there are exceptions: the platypus and spiny anteaters lay eggs! Marsupials, which include kangaroos, koalas, and opossums, give birth to embryo-like young that finish their development in their mother's pouch. All female mammals, however, do produce milk for their offspring. Because they nurse, young mammals spend a longer time with their mothers, a situation that offers them protection when they're most vulnerable, and an opportunity to learn survival skills.

■ Like other animals, each mammal fills a particular ecological place, or niche, and their bodies and behavior are suited to survive within it. A lion is built for stalking and chasing; a gazelle is built for speedy escapes; a hyena's teeth can crush bones; grazing animals have grinding molars; predators "think" with their noses, and nocturnal creatures have remarkable hearing ability.

■ Some mammals have "extended" niches, migrating seasonally along a particular route to better feeding grounds, or to breed. In regions with hard winters and a scarcity of food, animals that can't migrate to warmer areas often prepare by collecting food when it's plentiful and storing it for hard times. Others, like woodchucks, brown bats, and certain bears, put on a layer of fat before they shut down their metabolism to a near standstill and hibernate. Some mammals, like chipmunks, skunks, and raccoons are "light sleepers" who wake up to forage during milder winter days.

■ A mammal's brain has particularly large cerebral hemispheres which deal with consciousness and intelligence. Primates, dolphins, elephants, canids (dog family), and felids (cat family) are reputed to be among the most intelligent. But if you listen to a bear biologist, or read about amazingly clever wolverines, one can't help but be impressed by the resourceful abilities of mammals in general. Perhaps we're inclined to believe that they're the smartest animal class because we belong to the same group. We certainly find it easier to relate to them, and are able to "read" the body language and facial expressions of a mammal far better than we can those of a turtle or tuna! That's probably why dogs and cats continue to be the most popular pets, and why we're so comfortable sharing our lives with them.

STUDENT ACTIVITIES

All About Mammals

MATERIALS: reproducible page 15, pencil

This page, which your students can use as a handy guide, defines the characteristics that all mammals share and some that *most* of them share. Read it with the children and brainstorm examples as you go down the list. Ask them to name some animals and see if they meet the criteria: Do they breathe air? Do they provide milk for their babies? Do they have fur? When you think they understand what makes an animal a mammal, challenge them to circle the mammals on the page. **Answers:** *giant panda, gorilla, jaguar, mongoose, wolf*

EXTENSION: Conduct a class survey to find out what kinds of animals the children have at home. Are most of them mammals? Ask the children to describe something special about their pets.

Joey Pocket Puppet

MATERIALS: reproducible page 16, oaktag, paste, crayons, scissors, tape, craft stick

After distributing the necessary materials, help the children follow the instructions to assemble this simple puppet. When they're finished, they can hold their puppets by the craft stick and move the kangaroo as though it's jumping. Explain that kangaroos don't walk on all fours like most mammals. They get around in leaps and bounds—a large red kangaroo can travel 35 feet in one jump—so the joey gets some pretty bumpy rides! This can become a launching pad for discussions about the ways other mammals carry their young. Ask how lions carry their cubs (in their mouths), how anteaters carry their babies (on their backs), and how sea otters carry their young (on their bellies), etc.

Puppet Assembly Instructions:
1. Glue the puppet page to oaktag.
2. Color your joey and its mom then cut out parts A and B.
3. Cut just along the dashed line of the pouch on part A.
4. Slip the long end of part B into the pouch. Turn both parts over and fold the end of B to make a tab.
5. Tape a craft stick to part A so that it is parallel with the mother's tail. Now your Joey is ready to take a ride!

EXTRA: Have children do some research to discover where kangaroos live, what they eat, and how tall they can grow. Ask the children to write a kangaroo fact on a Post-it® Note and stick it on the puppet.

A Grizzly Puzzle
• • • • • • • • • • • • • • • • •

MATERIALS: reproducible page 17, scissors, oaktag, paste

Once your students fit the pieces of their puzzle togeth-

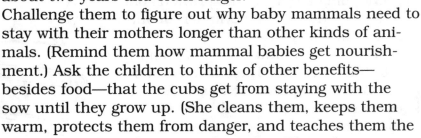

er, they'll see this picture of a grizzly mom (known as a sow) with her cubs. Let them know that cubs stay with their mom for about two years and often longer.

Challenge them to figure out why baby mammals need to stay with their mothers longer than other kinds of animals. (Remind them how mammal babies get nourishment.) Ask the children to think of other benefits—besides food—that the cubs get from staying with the sow until they grow up. (She cleans them, keeps them warm, protects them from danger, and teaches them the survival skills they'll need to have when they're on their own. The cubs are taught what to eat and what not to eat, how to hunt, how to dig, how to catch fish, and what animals to avoid.)

EXTRA: Have students make their own puzzles, using magazine photos, or pictures they've drawn.

Mixed-Up Tails
• • • • • • • • • • • • • • • • •

MATERIALS: reproducible page 18, construction paper, scissors, glue

As your students read the clues and restore the tails to their rightful owners, they'll discover that an animal's tail is a lot more than a fluffy add-on. They're used in a variety of ways: as steering rudders (beavers, seals, whales,); as balancing props (kangaroos, wallabies); as an extra limb (monkeys, lemurs); as a "blanket" (squirrels, foxes) and even as a toy (cats, dogs, monkeys). Tails are also used as signals: a skunk's raised tail warns other animals to move off or they will get sprayed; a deer signals danger to its herd by raising its white "flag."

Ask the children: What does a happy, friendly dog do with its tail? What does an unhappy or frightened dog do with its tail? What does a cat do with its tail when it greets you? How does a cat's tail look when it's angry or frightened?

If I Only Had a Tail

MATERIALS: 4 sheets of newspaper, scissors, sticky tape

Now that the children understand how useful a tail can be, they can make a luxurious tail of their own! Help them follow these four easy steps:

Tail Assembly Instructions:

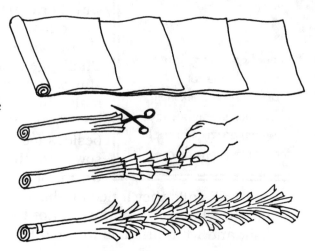

1. Open and lay out 4 pieces of (full size, large format) newspaper with each sheet overlapping a third of the previous one.
2. Roll them up into one cylinder (about 3 inches in diameter).
3. Hold at one end and cut a 5-6 inch fringe into the other end. The cuts should be about 1 inch apart. Use tape a few inches from the bottom to hold the tube together.
4. Reach into the middle, grip the innermost fringes, and pull. The fringed pages will "telescope" into a very showy tail!

Now the kids' imaginations will soar (or wag) to new heights! Encourage them to say aloud: If I only had a tail, I could . . . and finish the sentence. (Some six year olds suggested using it as an umbrella, a fan, a baton, a scarf, and a paint brush!)

EXTENSION: Have students write stories describing ways in which their new tails helped them out of a tricky situation.

Barnyard Scramble

MATERIALS: reproducible page 19, crayons

Here's a collection of familiar farm animals that even the youngest students will recognize. Ask them to unscramble the letters and write each animal's name in the box beneath it. Then they can color the picture.

EXTRA: Ask the children to tell you which of the animals "work" on the farm. What do they do?

Peek-Through Prairie Dog Town

MATERIALS: reproducible pages 20 and 21, crayons

Make double-sided copies of reproducible pages 20 and 21 for your students, and pass them out with page 20 up. As the children examine the desert scene and see the prairie dogs on bare mounds, explain that those are the "lookouts" and if one of them sees a predator such as a hawk, badger, or coyote, it utters a sharp bark, and all the prairie dogs quickly scamper into the burrows! Have the students read the information at the top of the page. Then, when they hold the page up to a light source, they'll discover the underground network of tunnels and escape routes.

Invite the children to turn the page over. They'll get an even better look at the hidden town and they can help Patsy the prairie dog find her way through the maze to her family.

Cat Cubes

MATERIALS: reproducible page 22, oaktag, scissors, glue, crayons, tape

A cat is a cat is a cat! Even our affectionate whiskered pets have the speed, grace, instincts, and hunting equipment of their larger wild relatives. Your students will clearly see similarities as they meet the wild felines on their Cat Cubes.

Give each student a set of cube patterns, and then help them follow these instructions:

Cube Assembly Instructions:
1. Paste this page to oaktag.
2. Color all the cats and then cut out both cube patterns.
3. Fold each pattern along the dotted lines to form a cube. Tuck the end flaps in and tape the edges to hold them together.

When the cubes are assembled, the children can move them around to match both ends of the cat pictures on the sides of the cubes.

Cat Family Fun Facts

- Cheetahs can run 60 mph, that is faster than the speed limit in most states!
- Tigers can grow over 9 feet long - not counting the tail!
- Lions are the only wild cats that live in large groups.
- Leopards spend more hours asleep than awake!

EXTRA: After they've matched the cubes correctly, challenge students to rearrange the cubes to create (and name) some fanciful feline "hybrids." You might even have students write something special about each one.

How Tall Is a Giraffe?

MATERIALS: rulers, pencils

The average giraffe can grow to be 20 feet tall. To help children visualize just how tall 20 feet is, try this activity. First, ask students to look around your classroom or their homes to find objects that are very familiar to them such as their desks, their favorite book, their favorite stuffed animal, or even their classmates. Once students have chosen their objects (or people), have them measure how tall they are. Then, challenge them to do the necessary math to figure out how many of these objects (or people) they would have to pile one on top of the other to be as tall as a giraffe. As students are measuring and experimenting, share the giraffe facts to the right with them.

Giraffe Fun Facts

- A newborn giraffe calf is six feet tall! When it's all grown up it may be 20 feet tall!
- A giraffe's long neck only has seven bones, just like other mammals.
- No two giraffes look exactly alike. Each one's fur has its own design as different as human fingerprints.

Sea-Mammal Wheel

MATERIALS: reproducible page 23, scissors, brass fastener, hole punch

This activity will remind your students that some mammals have adapted to life in the water, that not all of them have feet with paws and claws, and that some don't even have fur! Make a copy for each of the students, and help them follow these steps.

Wheel Assembly Instructions:
1. Cut the wheels out along the solid lines and use a hole punch to make the center holes.
2. Carefully cut out the windows in wheel A.
3. Place wheel A on top of wheel B and secure the two with a brass fastener.

Whale-Watch Match-Ups

MATERIALS: reproducible pages 24 and 25, scissors, crayons

Learning to distinguish different kinds of animals within the same order (a kangaroo from a koala, for example) is a lot easier than distinguishing individual animals of the same family (like a golden retriever from a yellow Lab)—but it still takes some doing! In this activity, students will sharpen their powers of observation as they sort and match the different whales on these cards. They'll also learn about the whales' sizes, colors, and diets.

Once you've made double-sided copies of the pages, the cards can be used in a number of ways. Younger children may enjoy:

1. Coloring the pictures according to the descriptions.
2. Cutting the pages along the dark solid lines into 8 whale cards.
3. Cutting each whale card in half along the dotted lines.
4. Mixing the pieces and then matching them correctly.

Older children can play Whale-Watcher which is fun for 2 to 4 players:
One set of 8 cards is placed on a table, picture side showing. Taking turns clockwise, each player asks the next player one question, such as: Which whale eats seals? Which whale is the longest? Which one is the Beluga whale? The challenged player points to the whale he or she thinks is the correct one. Each correct answer earns 3 points. The first player to reach 12 points is the winner.

Eloise the Elephant

MATERIALS: reproducible page 26, crayons, scissors, craft stick, tape

Distribute copies of Eloise the Elephant to each student and help them follow these steps.

Elephant Assembly Instructions:
1. Glue this page to a piece of oaktag.
2. Color parts A and B and cut them out. Then carefully cut the dashed line on part A.
3. Slip part B into the cut on part A.
4. Fold part B along the line and tape it to make a strong wiggle-tab.
5. Tape a craft stick to the back of part A.

As students experiment with making Eloise's ear flap, share the elephant facts to the right with them.

Elephant Fun Facts

- An elephant flaps its ears for a number of reasons: to flick away flies or birds, to make itself look bigger when charging other animals; and to cool itself off. The huge flat ears have many blood vessels close to the surface of the skin so when they're flapped through the air it lowers the temperature of the blood and cools the whole animal!
- An African bull elephant can weight more than 6 tons!
- A grown elephant eats over 300 pounds of plants every day.
- A newborn calf weighs more than 200 pounds!

BOOK BREAKS

The Leopard Son by Jackie Bell & Kit Carlson (McGraw Hill, 1996)

Otter On His Own by Doe Boyle (Smithsonian Oceanic Collection, 1995)

The Whales by Cynthia Rylant (Blue Sky/Scholastic, 1996)

If You Give a Moose a Muffin by Laura Numeroff (HarperCollins, 1991)

Animals Born Alive and Well by Ruth Heller (Grosset Dunlap, 1982)

Little Gorilla by Ruth Bornstein (Clarion Books, 1976)

The Mitten by Jan Brett (G.P. Putnam's Sons, 1989)

All About Mammals

Can you find the mammals below? Circle the animals you think are mammals. Use the clues in the center to help you.

gila monster

HOW TO SPOT A MAMMAL

1. **All** mammals have skeletons and backbones.
2. **All** mammals have lungs and breathe air.
3. **All** mammals produce milk for their babies.
4. **All** mammals are warm-blooded (can make their own body heat).
5. **Most** mammals have fur (except whales, dolphins, and a few others).
6. **Most** mammals give birth to live young (except for the platypus and spiny anteater who lay eggs).
7. **Most** mammals have four legs (except for some that spend most of their time in water and have flippers like whales, dolphins, and seals).

gorilla

giant panda

wolf

bumblebee

mongoose

jaguar

Joey Pocket Puppet

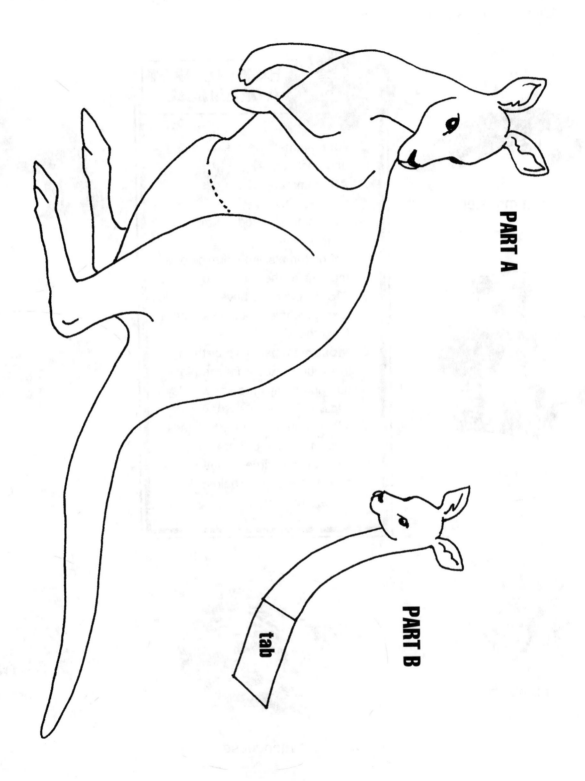

PART A

PART B

tab

NAME: _____

A Grizzly Puzzle

How many bears are there in this picture? To find out, cut out these puzzle pieces and shuffle them around to form a picture. Then if you want to, you can paste the picture onto oaktag and color it.

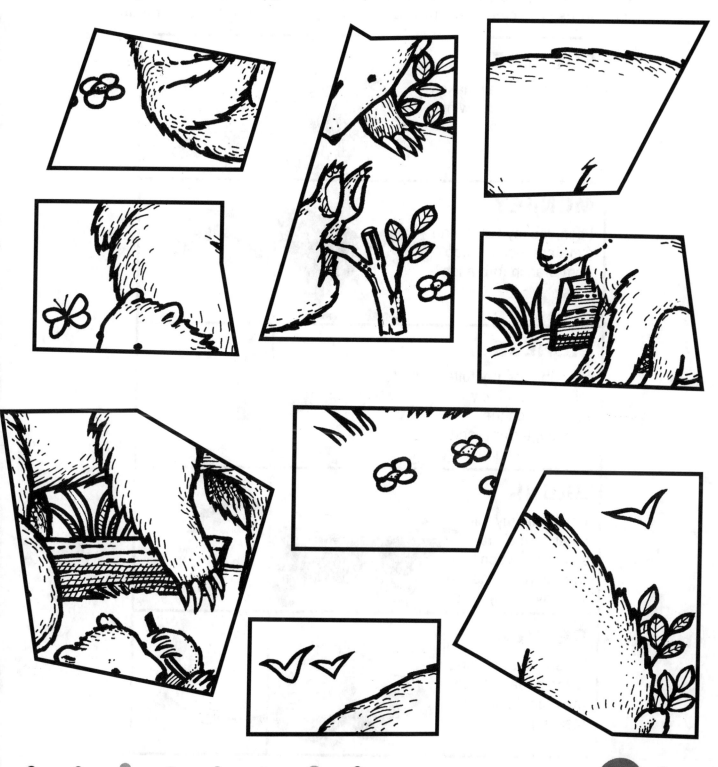

Mixed-Up Tails

Whoops! These mammals have their tails all mixed up! Can you help them get their own tails back? Cut the pictures out along the solid lines, then cut the tail sections off along the dotted lines. Paste the animals on a piece of construction paper and use the clues to help you put the right tail on the right animal.

SQUIRREL

My long fluffy tail makes a cozy blanket for winter naps.

MONKEY

I can use my tail like an extra arm when I leap from branch to branch.

LIONESS

My cubs use my tufted tail as a toy. They stalk it, then they pounce, tackle—and even chew on it.

SKUNK

When I lift my tail, other animals run away! They don't want to get splashed with my smelly spray!

BEAVER

When I'm swimming in the stream, I use my wide flat tail for steering.

NAME: _____

Barnyard Scramble

Can you unscramble the names of the nine mammals in this picture?

ACT
_____

OWC
_____

EHESP
_____

ROEHS
_____

TOGA
_____

BIBTAR
_____

IGP
_____

SUMOE
_____

DGO
_____

Peek-Through Prairie Dog Town

These plump mammals aren't dogs at all—they're rodents! There can be thousands of prairie dogs living in one town—but it's hidden! Below each mound is a tunnel with at least two or three ways in and out. To see what the underground town looks like, hold this page up to the light.

Nap Time for Patsy

Desert prairie dogs often take a nap during the hottest part of the day. It's nice and cool deep down in the tunnel, and Patsy wants to join her snoozing family. Can you help her find the way?

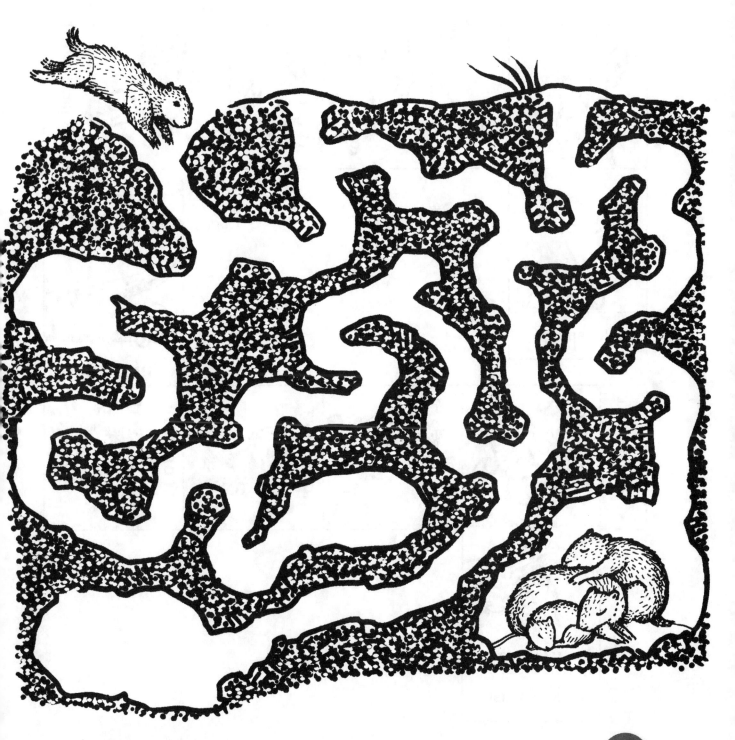

Cat Cubes

· · · · · · · · · · · · ·

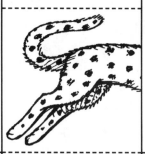

Tuck flap inside

Tuck flap inside

Tuck flap inside

Tuck flap inside

CHEETAH

Tuck flap inside

TIGER

LION

HOUSE CAT

LEOPARD

BOBCAT

Tuck flap inside

Sea-Mammal Wheel
• •

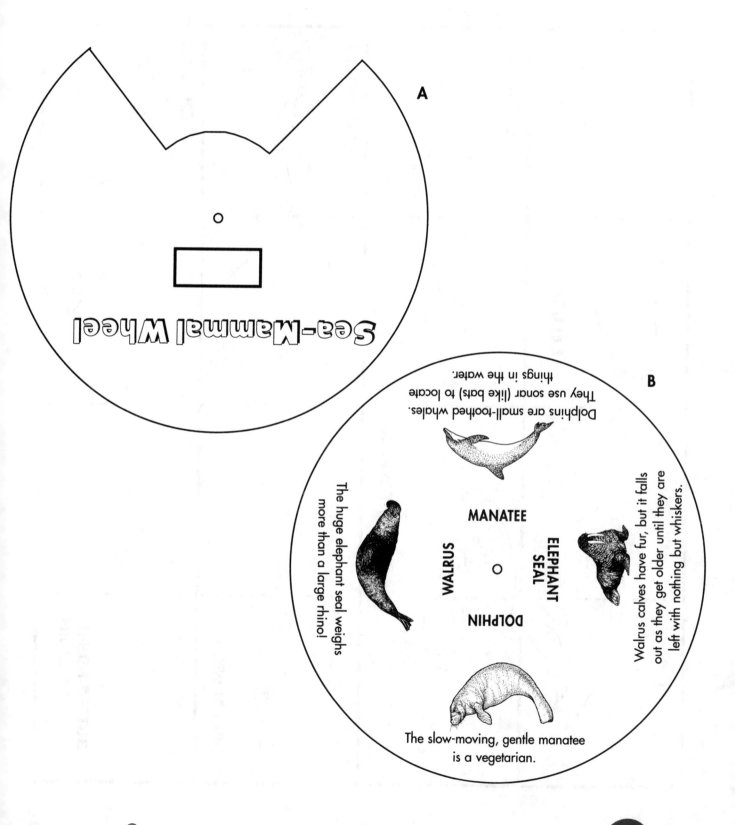

A

Sea-Mammal Wheel

B

Dolphins are small-toothed whales. They use sonar (like bats) to locate things in the water.

MANATEE

WALRUS

ELEPHANT SEAL

DOLPHIN

The huge elephant seal weighs more than a large rhino!

Walrus calves have fur, but it falls out as they get older until they are left with nothing but whiskers.

The slow-moving, gentle manatee is a vegetarian.

NAME: ______________________________

Whale-Watch Match-Ups (Front)

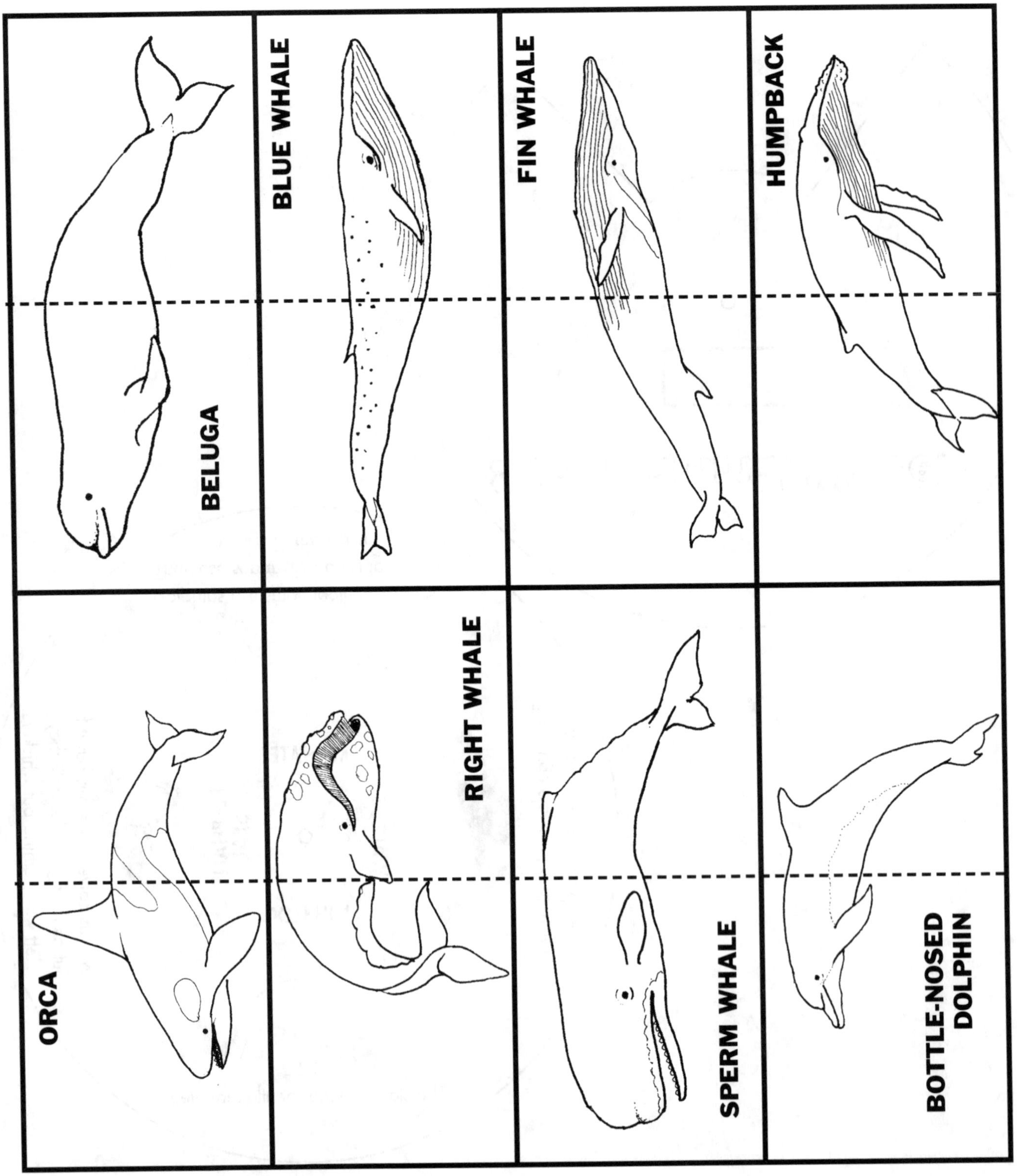
BELUGA
BLUE WHALE
FIN WHALE
HUMPBACK
ORCA
RIGHT WHALE
SPERM WHALE
BOTTLE-NOSED DOLPHIN

NAME: _____

Whale-Watch Match-Ups (Back)

HUMPBACK WHALE **Length:** up to 46 feet **Color:** black with white on its throat, belly, and flippers **Food:** fish and krill (tiny shrimp)	**FIN WHALE** **Length:** up to 80 feet **Color:** gray on back and white underneath **Food:** fish, krill (tiny shrimp), zooplankton (microscopic animals)	**BLUE WHALE** **Length:** up to 100 feet **Color:** spotty blue-gray **Food:** krill (tiny shrimp)	**BELUGA WHALE** **Length:** up to 16 feet **Color:** white **Food:** fish and zoo-plankton (microscopic animals)
BOTTLENOSE DOLPHIN **Length:** up to 13 feet **Color:** dark gray back, light gray on the sides, and white belly **Food:** squid, fish, octopi	**SPERM WHALE** **Length:** up to 55 feet **Color:** dark brown or gray with lighter mouth and head **Food:** squid, fish, octopi	**RIGHT WHALE** **Length:** up to 50 feet **Color:** black with white patches **Food:** zooplankton (microscopic animals)	**ORCA** **Length:** up to 30 feet **Color:** black and white **Food:** seals, fish, squid, birds, turtles, and other whales

Eloise the Elephant

A

B

CHAPTER 2

Living Fossils
Reptiles.......

BACKGROUND INFORMATION

Reptiles were once the most dominant creatures on earth. But the huge sea reptiles, flying pterosaurs, and giant turtles all died off with the dinosaurs 65 million years ago. Smaller reptiles then evolved. These are the ones we know today—except for the tuatara which, according to fossil evidence, hasn't changed for 200 million years! Of ordinary size and shape, the tuatara looks like an ordinary lizard at first, but a close inspection would reveal not only an extra row of teeth, but a third eye!

■ Reptiles all have an internal skeleton with a central backbone. They all breathe through lungs, are cold-blooded, and most are covered with horny scales or plates. The covering prevents their bodies from drying out, and makes it possible for reptiles to spend more of their time on land than amphibians. Some reptiles give birth to live young, but most lay eggs protected by shells.

■ Turtles comprise one group of reptiles, with about 300 species. Those that spend the greater part of their lives in water (often called terrapins) have flatter, lighter, and more streamlined shapes than the land dwelling species we know as tortoises. But flat or domed, their plated shells clearly set them apart from other kinds of reptiles.

■ Although more lizards can be found in the tropics, they actually inhabit all the continents except Antarctica. The lizard family includes iguanas, chameleons, and skinks, most of which have good vision; like snakes, lizards use their tongues to "taste" their surroundings. The 4,000 species range from a gecko barely an inch in length—to the 10 foot long Kimodo dragon!

■ Except for the salt-water crocodile, most crocodiles, alligators, caimans, and gharials live near tropical rivers and swamps. Most can be fearsome predators. The slender-snouted ones tend to dine on fish and frogs, but the strong, wide-snouted ones attack larger animals like cattle, antelopes, and zebras. A crocodile often loses some teeth chomping on those large dinners—but it doesn't matter because new ones continue to grow. Many crocodiles go through 50 or more sets of teeth in their lifetime.

■ Although most snakes are harmless and rather small, they're still feared by humans. Perhaps it's their speed and slithering motion that unnerves us; or maybe it's their unblinking stare. But what other method of locomotion could be more efficient for a legless animal with 400 vertebrae? And how can a snake be expected to stop staring when it has no eyelids?

■ Snakes have no outer ears, and although they have good vision, they usually detect prey by sensing its body heat, or tasting the air. The tongue is the most important sense-organ for most snakes. Its flickering tip picks up chemical traces from the surroundings and moves them to mouth pockets lined with chemo-receptors.

■ Although snakes can live for long stretches of time without eating, when they do eat, their meals are always other animals. Many eat mammals, birds, and insects, while others have highly specialized diets such as eggs, snails, or slugs.

STUDENT ACTIVITIES

All About Reptiles

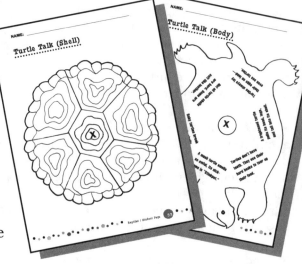

MATERIALS: reproducible page 32, pencil

Distribute copies of this reference page to your students and discuss the characteristics of reptiles with them. It's a good idea to point out the differences between reptiles and amphibians, because they're the most difficult animals to tell apart. For instance, a salamander (amphibian) looks a great deal like a gecko (reptile); a caecilian (amphibian) closely resembles a thread snake (reptile). The most obvious clue for the students is the creature's covering—reptiles have dry scaly skin and plates while amphibians have soft, moist skin. Ask the children what they think a snake feels like? Would it be slimy? (No, it feels dry and muscular.) What does a turtle shell feel like? (Like hard plastic.) Name a few common animals (cat, skunk, sparrow) and ask why they can't be reptiles. When you think your students understand what makes a reptile a reptile, have them circle the reptiles on the page. **Answers:** *anaconda, chuckwalla, crocodile, hawksbill, thorny devil.*

Turtle Talk

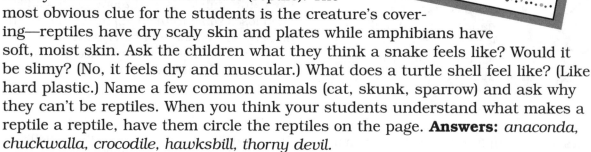

MATERIALS: reproducible pages 33 and 34, crayons, scissors, glue

Here's a fun way for your students to discover a lot of fascinating facts about turtles. Distribute copies of the reproducible pages to each student and ask the children to color the turtle's head, feet, tail, and shell (on the second page). Have them cut the shell out along the scalloped edges and along the flap lines. When that's done, have them put a little bit of glue in the circle with the "x" and place the shell on top so it adheres only in the very center. As the children lift the flaps, ask them to read the turtle facts aloud, and compare them with other kinds of animals. For instance, when they read about how the turtle draws into its shell to protect itself, ask how other animals defend themselves. How do they think a skunk defends itself? (spray) An ostrich? (speed, powerful kicks) A lion? (speed, teeth, claws)

Reptile Triplets

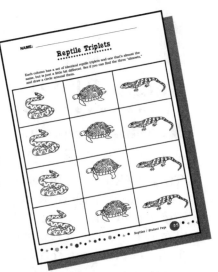

MATERIALS: reproducible page 35, pencil

Challenge the students' powers of observation with this activity! Can they find the snake, turtle, and lizard that is just a *little* different from the look-alike triplets?

Snake Snooping

MATERIALS: reproducible page 36, pencil

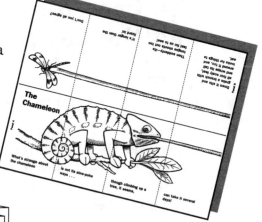

What kind of snake is this? Ask students to imagine that they are snake experts and that someone has brought a snake to them to identify. Distribute a copy of reproducible page 36 to each student and have them compare the mystery snake to the other snakes in their "collection". Once students have identified the snake, ask them to do some research to answer the questions at the bottom of their report page. Be sure to have plenty of snake books on hand. If you do not have access to lots of resources, encourage children to take turns doing their research.

The Chameleon

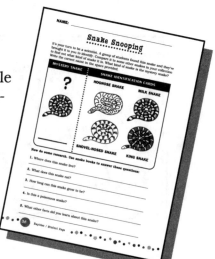

MATERIALS: reproducible page 37, scissors, tape

Ask your students what they think is strange about a chameleon. Is it the way it looks? Is it what it eats? Invite students to assemble this fanned mini-book to discover a fascinating fact about chameleons. (Their tongues are longer than their bodies!)

Mini-Book Assembly Instructions:
1. Cut the page in half along the solid line.
2. Align the end of panel A with the beginning of panel B and then tape the two parts together along the back with no overlap.
3. Then fold along the dotted lines in alternate directions as illustrated.

Gecko Glider

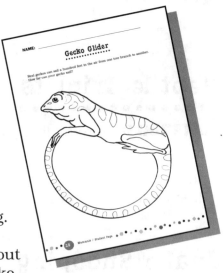

MATERIALS: reproducible page 38, colored markers, oaktag, glue, scissors

This gecko can glide almost as far as the real one! Give each student a copy of reproducible page 38. First they should glue the page to a piece of oaktag. Then have them color their geckos leaf green with bright red spots. Lastly, they should carefully cut out their geckos. As students are assembling their gecko gliders, you may want to discuss the gecko fun facts below with them.

Gecko Fun Facts

- Geckos are the only reptiles that make lots of sounds—they squeak, chirp, quack, croak, bark, and even call "gecko".
- Geckos can run upside-down on a ceiling.
- People like geckos because they eat lots of insects.

Once students have made their gliders, have them practice tossing them like a Frisbee™ holding onto the gecko's head. Then, hold a contest to see how far the class geckos can glide. Older students can use a measuring tape or a yardstick to measure their gecko's distance.

The Crocodile and the Capybaras

MATERIALS: reproducible page 39, oaktag, crayons, scissors, glue, pennies

To make this board game, ask the children to cut out the capybaras, then paste the rest of the sheet onto oaktag. Students can color the animals. Next, have the students cut out the capybara circles and glue each one to a penny (for easy tossing). Explain that capybaras are the largest rodents in the world. They can weigh up to 100 pounds! They're gentle vegetarians who enjoy swimming in rain forest rivers—*but so do dangerous crocodiles!* The object of the game is to land in the river without becoming a crocodile's lunch! Each child can stand at a "throw line" and try to toss his or her capybaras so they land in a safe rectangle. Each player starts with 12 points (three tosses). Each time they land in a safe rectangle they win a point, and each time they land on a crocodile, they loose a point. The player with the highest score after 5 tosses is the winner.

As Lo-o-o-ng as a Reptile

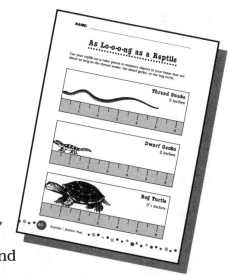

MATERIALS: reproducible pages 40 and 41, scissors

Have students cut out the reptile-on-a-ruler pieces to complete this treasure hunt. Students will sharpen their measurement skills as they hunt through their homes to find objects the same size as a thread snake, a dwarf gecko, and a bog turtle. Have students record their findings and bring them back to class to share and compare with others.

Slithery-Snake Mobile

MATERIALS: reproducible page 42, crayons or markers, scissors, string

Have students create a slithering snake of their own. Distribute a copy of page 42 to each student. Invite students to decorate their snake with bright colors and fanciful patterns. Once they have colored their snakes, have students cut them out along the solid lines. Help students assemble their mobiles by punching a hole through the end of their snakes to pull the string through. Ask students to give their snakes names and share some imaginary fun facts about them (i.e., what they eat, where they live, etc.).

BOOK BREAKS

Snakes by Kate Petty (Franklin Watts, 1990)

I Wonder Why Snakes Shed Their Skin by Amanda O'Neill (Kingfisher, 1996)

Snakes by Stoops & Wright (Sterling Publishers, 1994)

Sea Turtle Journey by Lorraine Jay (Smithsonian Institute, 1995)

All About Reptiles

Can you find the reptiles below? Circle the animals you think are reptiles. Use the clues in the center to help you.

anaconda

chuckwalla

HOW TO SPOT A REPTILE

1. **All** reptiles are cold-blooded (their temperature is the same as their surroundings).
2. **All** reptiles have skeletons with backbones.
3. **All** reptiles breathe air.
4. **All** reptiles are covered with *scales* or *plates*.
5. **Reptiles** live in deserts, oceans, forests, and jungles, but can't live in very cold climates.
6. **Most** reptiles shed their skins as they grow bigger.
7. **Most** reptile babies hatch from eggs.
8. **Reptile** babies can feed themselves.

crocodile

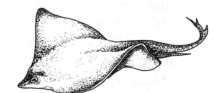

stingray

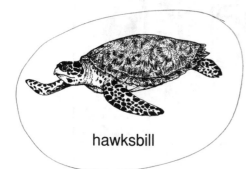

hawksbill

flying frog

thorny devil

Turtle Talk (Shell)

Turtle Talk (Body)

Not all turtle shells are hard. Some are soft like leather.

Turtles always lay their eggs on land—even sea turtles.

A frightened turtle pulls its head, legs, and tail into its shell.

Baby turtles break out of their shells with an "egg beak."

Turtles don't have teeth. They use their hard beaks to tear up their food.

A musk turtle smells so awful, its nick-name is "Stinkpot."

NAME: _____

Reptile Triplets
• • • • • • • • • • • • • • • • • • • •

Each column has a set of identical reptile triplets and one that's almost the same, but is just a little bit different. See if you can find the three "almosts," and draw a circle around them.

NAME: _____

Snake Snooping

It's your turn to be a scientist. A group of students found this snake and they've brought it to you to identify. Compare it to some other snakes in your collection to find out what kind of snake it is. What kind of snake is the mystery snake? Write the correct name in the space provided.

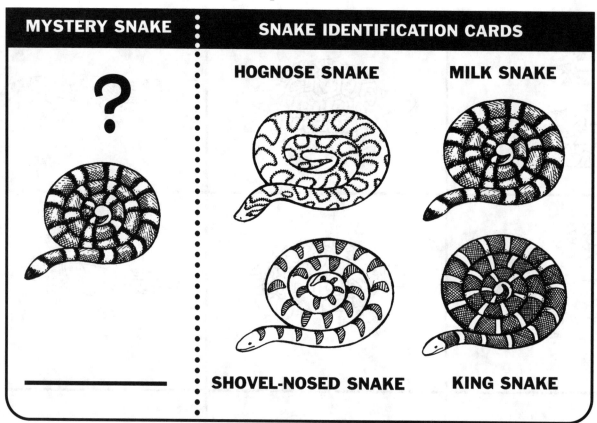

Now do some research. Use snake books to answer these questions:

1. Where does this snake live?

_____

2. What does this snake eat?

_____

3. How long can this snake grow to be?

_____

4. Is this a poisonous snake?

_____

5. What other facts did you learn about this snake?

_____

The Chameleon

What's strange about the chameleon

is not its slow-poke ways . . .

though climbing up a tree, it seems,

can take it several days!

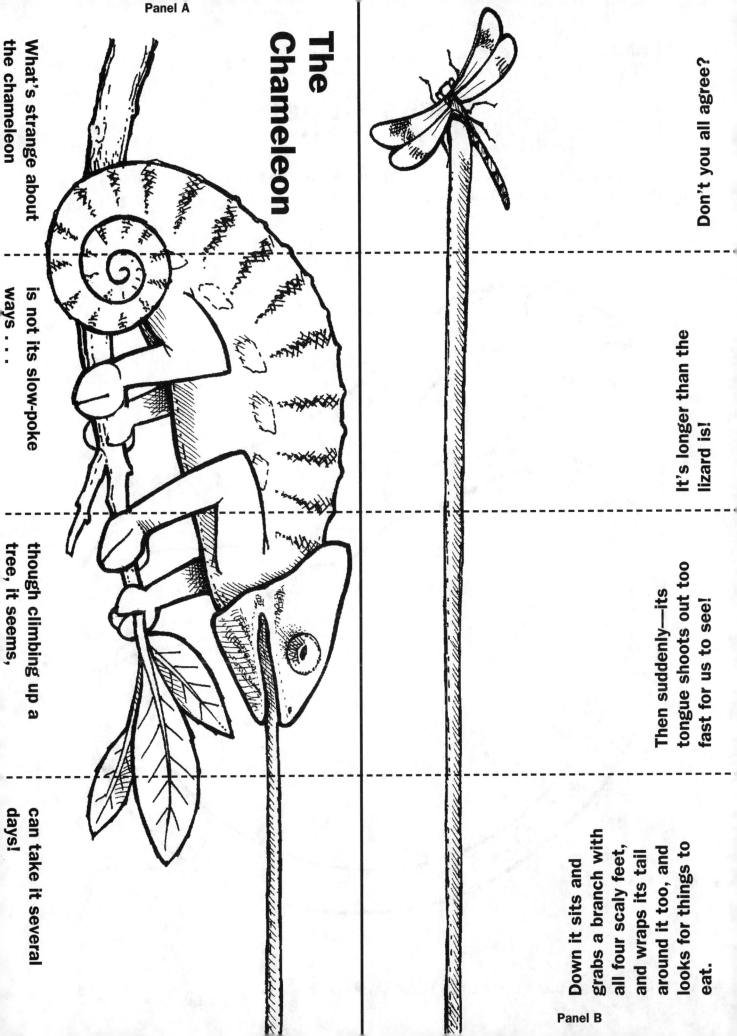

Don't you all agree?

It's longer than the lizard is!

Then suddenly—its tongue shoots out too fast for us to see!

Down it sits and grabs a branch with all four scaly feet, and wraps its tail around it too, and looks for things to eat.

Gecko Glider

Real geckos can sail a hundred feet in the air from one tree branch to another. How far can your gecko sail?

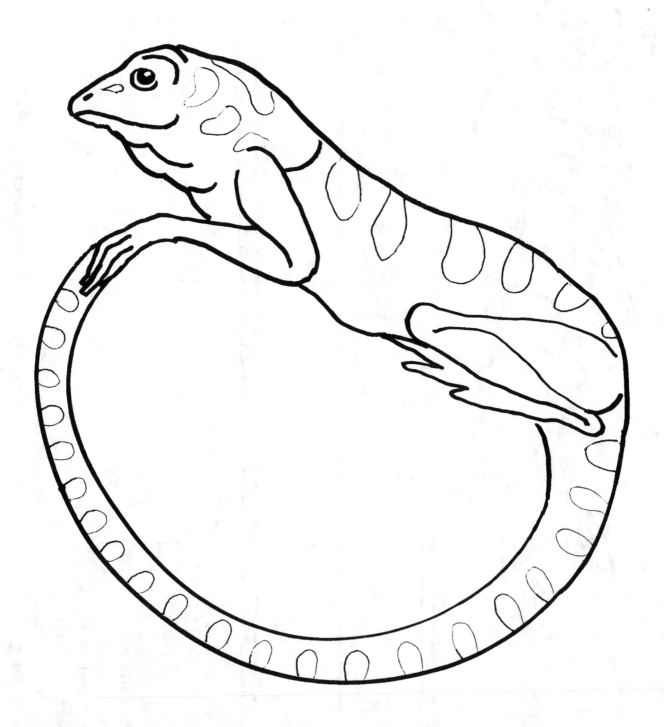

The Crocodile and the Capybaras

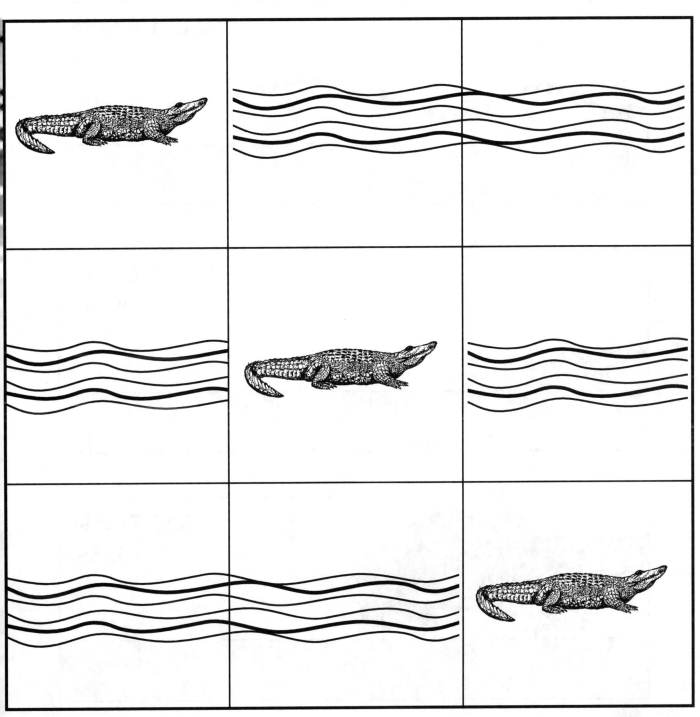

As Lo-o-o-ng as a Reptile

Use your reptile-on-a-ruler pieces to measure objects in your home that are about as long as the thread snake, the dwarf gecko, or the bog turtle.

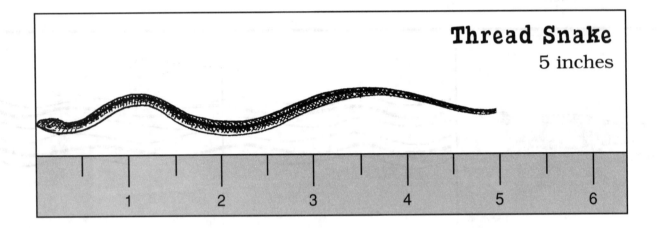

Thread Snake
5 inches

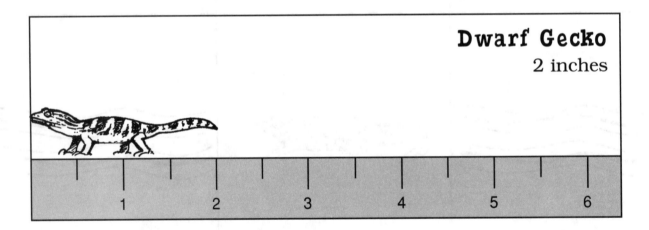

Dwarf Gecko
2 inches

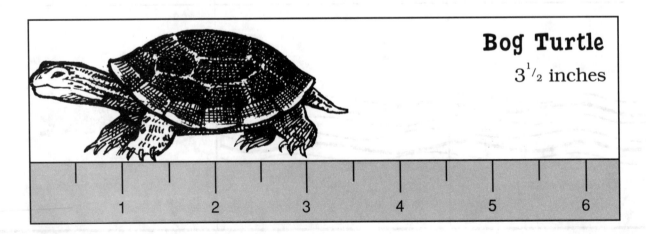

Bog Turtle
$3\frac{1}{2}$ inches

As Lo-o-o-ng as a Reptile

Here are things I found that are about the same length as the thread snake:

_____

_____

_____

Here are things I found that are about the same length as the dwarf gecko:

_____

_____

_____

Here are things I found that are about the same length as the bog turtle:

_____

_____

_____

Slilthery-Snake Mobile

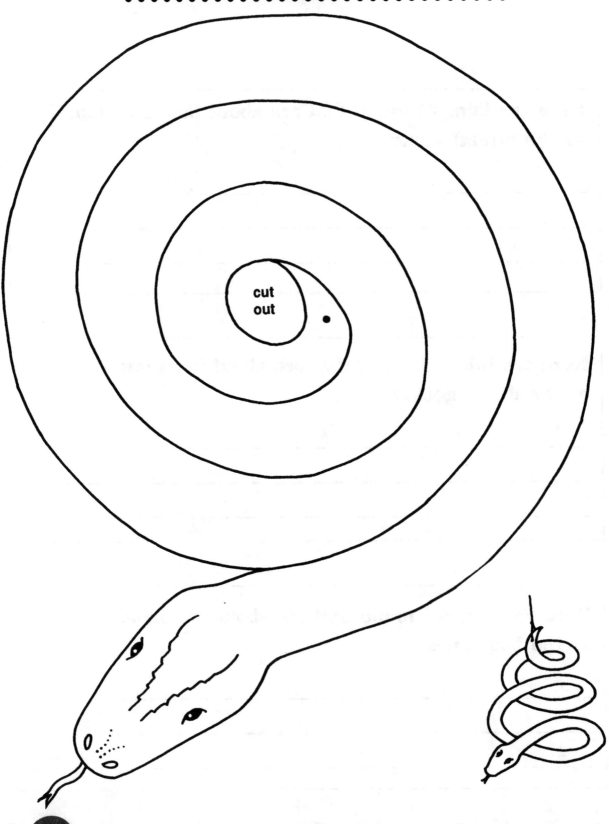

cut
out

CHAPTER 3

Double Lives
Amphibians......

BACKGROUND INFORMATION

The name amphibian comes from the Greek words: amphi and bios, meaning double life. It refers to the fact that most amphibians spend part of their lives in water, and part on land. The class includes frogs, toads, newts, salamanders, mudpuppies, and the least known, strange, worm-like, caecilians.

■ The oldest amphibian fossils are 360 million years old, and show that many of the ancient species were thirteen feet long! They ruled the earth for a long time, until they were dethroned by other newly evolved reptilian animals—dinosaurs.

■ There's often confusion between amphibians and reptiles because so many reptiles, like alligators and turtles, also spend a good deal of time in water. Amphibians, however, always spend the early part of their lives in water, breathing through gills, and looking much more like fish than like their parents. However, as the larvae develop, their bodies change dramatically, and after growing legs, lungs, and mouths for eating insects, they're ready for life on land.

■ Amphibians are vertebrates, meaning that they have a backbone and an internal skeleton. Most have hands with four fingers and feet with five toes. They're ectothermic, or cold-blooded, so their body temperature depends upon the temperature of their surroundings. Unlike scaly reptiles, amphibians usually have soft skin that can dry out quickly, so they tend to live in damp places. They also have glands in their skin which produce a slimy mucus to help keep them moist.

■ Their soft skin and small size would make most adult amphibians tempting meals for a number of mammals, birds, reptiles, and even larger amphibians, were it not for their poison-producing glands. Some species, usually the brightly colored ones, are highly toxic with poisons that can kill a predator rapidly. But even the non-lethal amphibians taste awful!

■ Your class will be delightfully surprised at the wonderful variety and amazing abilities of these half-and-half creatures.

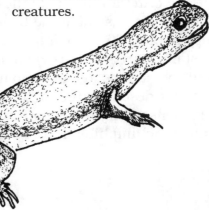

STUDENT ACTIVITIES

All About Amphibians

MATERIALS: reproducible page 49, pencil

After you distribute copies of this reference page to your students and review the three groups of amphibians (frogs/toads, salamanders/newts, and caecilians), it's a good idea to offer examples, and to brainstorm comparisons with reptiles—the animals most often confused with amphibians. Although most amphibians spend part of their lives in water and part on land, students might point out that crocodiles (who are reptiles), for instance, do the same thing! Use the crocodile as an example to clarify the criteria. Does it have a backbone and skeleton? Yes. Does it have skin without fur, scales, or feathers? Yes. Is it cold-blooded? Yes. But does it have soft skin? No! So it cannot be an amphibian! After your students are comfortable with the defining characteristics, ask them to circle the amphibians on the page. **Answers:** *caecilian, newt, salamander spadefoot, spring peeper.*

Amphib-A-Riddle Flap Book

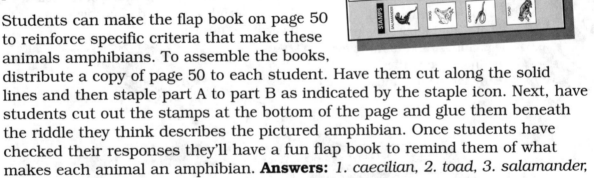

MATERIALS: reproducible page 50, scissors, paste

Students can make the flap book on page 50 to reinforce specific criteria that make these animals amphibians. To assemble the books, distribute a copy of page 50 to each student. Have them cut along the solid lines and then staple part A to part B as indicated by the staple icon. Next, have students cut out the stamps at the bottom of the page and glue them beneath the riddle they think describes the pictured amphibian. Once students have checked their responses they'll have a fun flap book to remind them of what makes each animal an amphibian. **Answers:** *1. caecilian, 2. toad, 3. salamander, 4. frog.*

The Tale of a Tadpole

MATERIALS: reproducible pages 51 and 52, scissors

Your students will grasp the sequential events of an amphibian's development when they make this mini-book. Begin by providing each child with a double-sided photocopy of pages 51 and 52. Be sure that both sides feature the same top/bottom orientation. Students can assemble their book by following these steps:

1. Cut the book out along the solid lines.

2. Fold all four corners toward the center along the dashed lines, covering the pictures.

3. Fold to form a triangle with the title showing.

4. Then lift the numbered flaps clockwise, to show the developing stages of an amphibian.

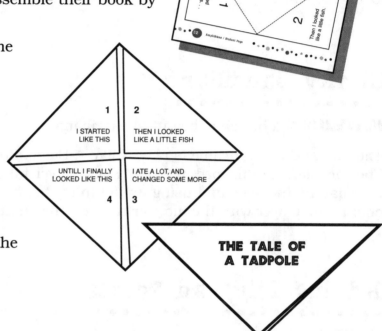

Cecily Caecilian

MATERIALS: reproducible page 53, paste, scissors, scraps of colorful gift-wrap or scraps of magazine pictures

It's always fun to find an exception to the rule—so here's Cecily, an amphibian with no legs, who looks more like a snake or a big worm! She's fun to make, and can be used in a number of ways. Start by having the children cut out snips of colorful pictures from old magazines and flyers then give each one a copy of reproducible page 53. Help students follow these directions to make their caecilian:

1. Cut out the picture of Cecily Caecilian.

2. Paste the brightly colored strips of paper to one side. (Do not worry if they hang over the edge.)

3. Once the glue has dried, trim off all the excess paper.

4. Glue the rest of the brightly colored scraps of paper to her other side.

5. Trim all the excess paper off Cecily.

6. Make eyes by cutting little circles out of white paper and then glue them on.

When all the caecilians are completed, the children can use them to play the following game.

Slinky Caecilians
• • • • • • • • • • • • • • • •

MATERIALS: a bunch of beautiful caecilians

The Slinky Caecilian game is played like A Barrel Full of Monkeys:
The caecilians are heaped in a pile. Each player takes a turn by picking up one caecilian by the neck and using its tail to try to lift another caecilian onto the chain. The player with the most critters on the chain is the winner.

Adding Lily Pad Points
• •

MATERIALS: reproducible pages 54 and 55, oaktag, glue, crayons, scissors

This activity can be geared to your students' math level in a variety of ways. The simplest game is on reproducible page 54. All students need to do is glue the frog pictures to a piece of oaktag, color them and then write their name in the space provided. Then they should cut out the frogs to use as playing pieces. Next, cut out the lily pads and place them randomly on a desk or table top. Have students take turns tossing their frog pieces onto the lily pads. Once all three pieces have been thrown, students add their lily pad points. The student with the most points wins. You can make the game more complex by having the students add their first two landings and subtracting the third, and so forth.

Hopping Homer

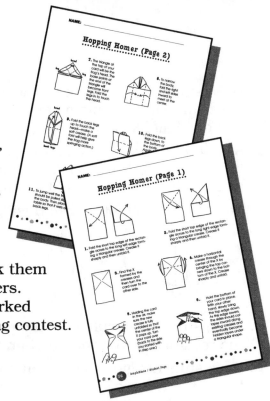

MATERIALS: reproducible pages 56 and 57, 3" x 5" unlined index cards, pencil

Here's an origami frog that really jumps! It's a little tricky to make the first time, so the students may need some time to practice.

After the students have made their frogs ask them to write their initials on their Hopping Homers. Prepare an area with a starting line and marked measurements, and then hold a frog jumping contest.

Hop to It!

Ask the children to think of kinds of animals that hop rather than walk. (Many birds are "hoppers," as well as a whole bunch of insects and mammals.) Frogs and toads are hoppers—at least on land. Why is hopping an efficient way for some creatures to get around? Ask the children if they think people could get around faster by hopping? Form relay teams, establish a starting line (which is also the finish line). Have each team member hop (on both feet) from the starting line to a marked area where they turn and hop back to the starting point before the next hopper starts. Repeat the relay race with the teams walking quickly or skipping rather than hopping. Have them compare the results. Were they what the students expected?

Pop-Up Salamander Book

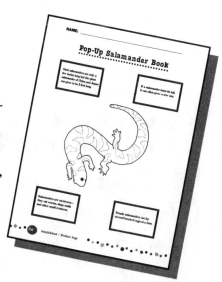

MATERIALS: reproducible page 58, crayons or markers, construction paper, scissors, glue

Here's a fun- and fact-filled pop-up book to teach your students about salamanders. To make the book, distribute a copy of reproducible page 58, and the necessary art supplies to each student. Then just follow these simple steps:

1. Invite students to color their salamanders and cut them out.

2. Have students cut the construction paper in half horizontally, and then fold one half like a book.

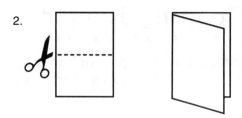

3. Ask students to draw a rectangle one inch high and three inches long on the spare half of paper and cut it out.

4. Then have them fold it like this:

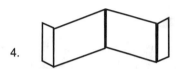

5. Next, students should glue the ends of the rectangle to the construction paper.

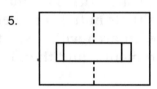

6. Have students glue their salamander's tail to the rectangle.

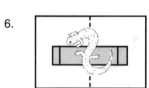

7. Once students have assembled their pop-up salamander, have them cut the fact boxes from the reproducible and glue them to the inside of the book.

Invite students to come up with a title for their book and have them design a cover. You might even suggest that they add some salamander facts of their own to the book's interior.

BOOK BREAKS

Frogs and Toads by Kate Petty (Franklin Watts, 1985)

Frogs Are Fantastic by Robin Robbins (Joshua Morris Books, 1995)

Jump, Frog, Jump! by Robert Kalan (Mulberry Books, 1981)

NAME: _____

All About Amphibians

Can you find the amphibians below? Circle the animals you think are amphibians. Use the clues in the center to help you.

spring peeper

HOW TO SPOT AN AMPHIBIAN

1. **All** amphibians have backbones and skeletons.
2. **All** amphibians have skin without fur, scales, or feathers.
3. **All** amphibians are cold-blooded (cannot make their own body heat).
4. **All** amphibians have soft skin.
5. **Most** amphibians hatch from eggs laid in water.
6. **Most** amphibians have lungs, but can also take in air through their skin.
7. **Most** amphibians live part of their lives in water, and part on land.
8. **Most** adult amphibians have poison producing glands that make them taste bad or might even kill a predator.

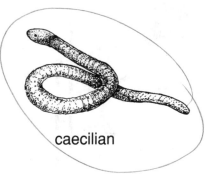

caecilian

spadefoot

salamander

shark

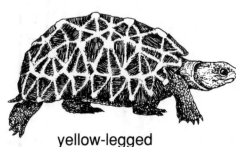

yellow-legged tortoise

newt

My Amphib-A-Riddle Flap Book

What am I?
1

I may look like a worm to you,
but no worm's as fast as me.
By the time you say my name,
I'm gone! I'm history!

What am I?
2

Don't confuse me with my cousin—
that makes me downright grumpy.
Anyone can clearly see I'm more
handsome—and more bumpy!

What am I?
3

I look much like a lizard does,
especially with this tail—
but if you hold me right up close,
you won't find a single scale!

What am I?
4

My skin is green and slippery,
my back legs long and strong.
And if you're out some summer night,
you'll get to hear my song!

| paste stamp here |
| paste stamp here |
| paste stamp here |
| paste stamp here |

STAMPS

SALAMANDER

FROG

CAECILIAN

TOAD

NAME: _____

The Tale of a Tadpole (Front)

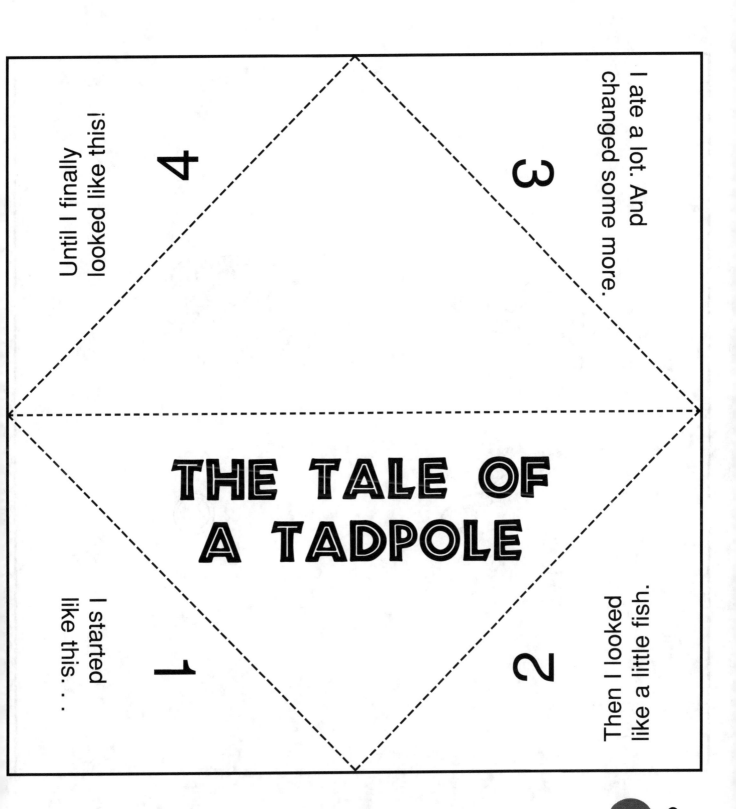

3

I ate a lot. And changed some more.

4

Until I finally looked like this!

THE TALE OF A TADPOLE

1

I started like this. . .

2

Then I looked like a little fish.

The Tale of a Tadpole (Back)

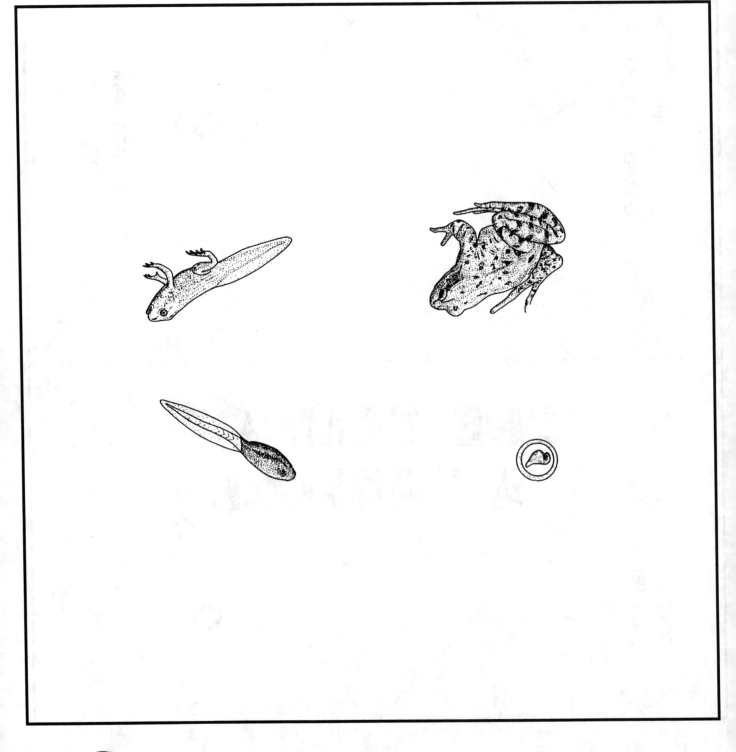

Cecily Caecilian

When you finish decorating Cecily, you can hang her on the wall, you can use her as a bookmark, or even a fun toy!

Adding Lily Pad Points (Frogs)

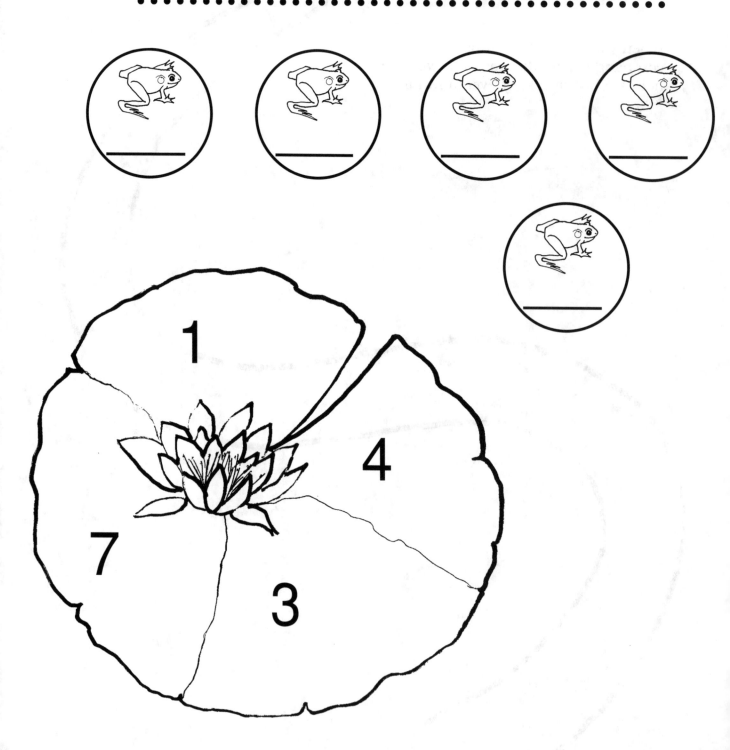

Adding Lily Pad Points

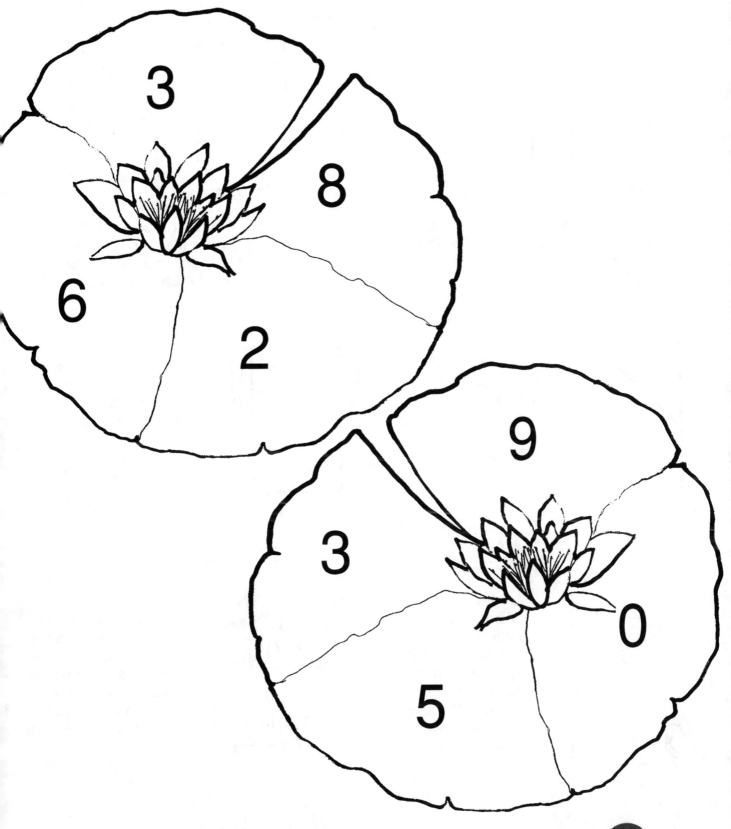

Hopping Homer (Page 1)

1. Fold the short top edge of the rectangle across to the long left edge forming a triangular crease. Crease it sharply and then unfold it.

2. Fold the short top edge of the rectangle across to the long right edge forming a triangular crease. Crease it sharply and then unfold it.

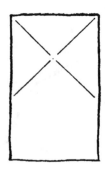

3. Find the X formed by the creases and then turn the card over to the other side.

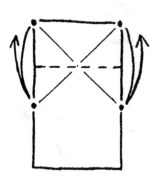

4. Make a horizontal crease through the center of the X by bringing the top corners down to the bottom of the X. Crease sharply and unfold.

5. Holding the card in the air, make sure the new crease is fully unfolded so that the center of the X pops up. Turn your card over (back to the side you started with in step one.)

6. Hold the bottom of your card in place. With your other hand, slowly bring the top edge down. As this edge lowers, the sides should collapse inward along existing creases and eventually become hidden layers under a triangular shape.

Hopping Homer (Page 2)

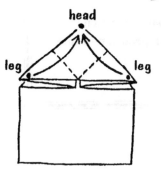

7. The triangle at the top of your card will be the frog's head. The loose points at the end of the triangle will become front legs. Fold the legs in to touch the head.

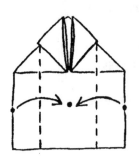

8. To narrow the body, fold the right and left sides inward to meet at the center.

9. Fold the back legs up to touch the head—make a soft crease. (A soft fold will help give the frog more springing action.)

10. Fold the back legs down, to the bottom of the body. Again fold *softly*, not sharply.

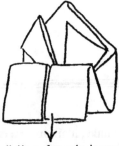

11. To jump well the frog's back legs should be pulled slightly away from the body. Then place your frog on a table so that it rests on its front and back legs.

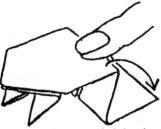

12. Press the frog's rear folded edge over the back legs and down to the table. Let your finger slide off the rear edge with a snap and your frog will jump!

Pop-Up Salamander Book

Most salamanders are only a few inches long but the giant salamander of China and Japan can grow to be 5 feet long.

If a salamander loses its tail, it can often grow a new one.

Salamanders are carnivores—they eat worms, slugs, snails and other small creatures.

Female salamanders can lay several hundred eggs at a time.

CHAPTER 4

Life in the Deep
Fish

BACKGROUND INFORMATION

Until the sixteenth century practically anything found swimming in water was considered a fish! Natural historians not only classified crocodiles, turtles, and crabs as fish, but also aquatic mammals such as whales, seals, otters, and even hippopotamuses!

■ As knowledge broadened, definitions narrowed. Today fish are described as cold-blooded, water-dwelling animals with flexible back-bones; they have fins, are usually covered with scales, and breath through gills. And there are lots of them—more in sheer mass than birds, mammals, and reptiles put together! The 25,000 species fall into two basic types: the majority with bony structure, and the rest with cartilaginous structure, like sharks and rays. The delicious food we refer to as "shellfish" isn't fish at all! Lobsters, crabs, and shrimp are crustaceans, while clams, mussels, squid, and oysters are mollusks.

■ Fish are a major food source for other fish, seabirds, reptiles, many land mammals, including humans, and even some kinds of voracious insect larvae! But fish are also predatory and have developed some successful (and bizarre) methods to catch their food. The little archer fish likes to eat flying insects, so it pokes its snout above the water's surface and shoots water at a potential meal. With a single well-aimed shot, it can bring down a moth, a spider—even a small lizard! Another fish with an unusual ability is the mudskipper, who can remain out of water for prolonged periods of time and often chases down insects by hopping after them like a frog!

■ Fish live nearly everywhere—from the deepest seas to lakes high in the mountains. They range in size from half an inch to over sixty feet, and some of their behavior is surprisingly mammal or bird-like: Certain species devote considerable effort to caring for their young; many use camouflage, build "nests," ambush their prey, use lures, have social structure, and migrate. But what bird or mammal can make its own light or produce electricity?!

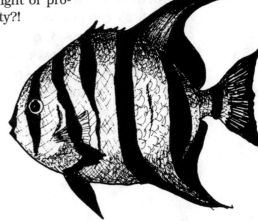

STUDENT ACTIVITIES

All About Fish

MATERIALS: reproducible page 65, pencil

Give your students a few minutes to look over this reference sheet, then review the characteristics of fish with them. Explain that many creatures living in the sea aren't necessarily fish. Name some excellent swimmers, like otters, seals, and alligators. Challenge the students to figure out why those animals aren't fish. What about whales and dolphins? They both look like fish, they spend their lives in the sea, so why aren't they fish? When you think students understand the defining characteristics, ask them to circle the fish on the page. **Answers:** *carp, pirahna, sawfish, shark, starfish.*

What Samuel Seahorse Saw

MATERIALS: reproducible pages 66 and 67, scissors, crayons

This mini-book tells the story of an adventurous young seahorse and the fish he meets on his journey. Make double-sided copies of pages 66 and 67 for each of your students so that the title page and page 2 are back-to-back. Have students cut the page apart along the solid lines, and stack the portions with the title page on top, followed by pages 3, 5, and 7. Finally, students should fold the pages down the dotted line and staple them along the spine. Invite the children to color their books after reading the story.

Sea Animal Names

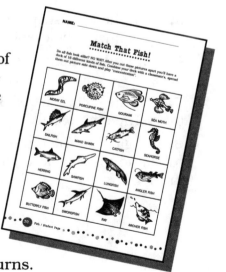

MATERIALS: reproducible page 68, pencil

Distribute copies of this activity to your students, and remind them that sea animals come in as many shapes as land animals. And like many mammals and birds, they often have names based on their appearance. Ask the children to read the names in the word box and write them under the correct picture. After students have told why they believe each creature is named as it is, encourage them to invent and share new names for these creatures.

Pufferfish Puzzle

MATERIALS: reproducible page 69, pencil

Distribute copies of the crossword puzzle on reproducible page 69 to help your students learn more about life in the water. **Answers:** *Across: 1. water 2. shark 4. tail 5. eyes 8. fins 10. eel; Down: 1. whale 2. salmon 3. cat 6. scales 7. reefs 9. seal*

Match That Fish!

MATERIALS: reproducible page 70, oaktag, paste, scissors

After the children have a chance to look at the variety of fish on the page, suggest that they color the fish, paste the page to a piece of oaktag for durability, and cut the pictures apart to form playing cards. By combining their decks, two students can play "concentration." To play, they need to spread the cards on a flat surface, and mix them face down. A coin toss can determine who plays first. Player A picks a card, turns it over in place and picks a second card, trying to match it. If it isn't a match, both cards are left where they are, but turned face down again. If a player gets a match, he or she keeps the set. In either case, players alternate turns. The winner is the player with the most sets of fish cards.

Squiggley-Squid

MATERIALS: reproducible page 71, scissors, tape, 12-14" newspaper edge, glue stick

Tell your students that squids aren't fish but mollusks, and are related to octopuses. Most are about the size of the Squiggley Squid on page 71, but some grow to be over 50 feet long! They have 10 tentacles (2 of which are much longer than the others) surrounding their mouths. Large groups of squid swim quickly after small fish, but when bigger fish (or penguins or seals) chase them, squids often release a cloud of "ink," which gives them some time to escape.

Here's an easy paper squid that looks like the real thing! Give each child a copy of page 71, and help them follow these steps:

Squiggley-Squid Assembly Instructions

1. Cut the paper along the dark solid lines, and discard part C.

2. Fold part A along the dotted lines.

3. Roll part A into a tube. Tape the seam, be careful not to cover the eyes.

4. Cut the strip of newspaper border lengthwise to make 2 long strips that are 1/2 inch wide.

5. Glue the long strips inside the tube (near the eyes).

6. Cut part B along the solid lines.

7. Roll the solid part of B into a tube. Tape it closed.

8. Put glue on the top of the B tube and insert it into part A (near the eyes).

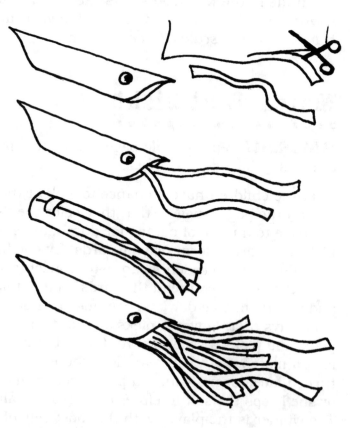

Where's Oscar?

MATERIALS: reproducible page 72, blue crayon

Hidden in this activity is one of children's favorite animals, a giant octopus!

After students find all the even numbers on the page and color the sections they appear in blue, have them turn the page upside down to find Oscar.

Racing Downstream

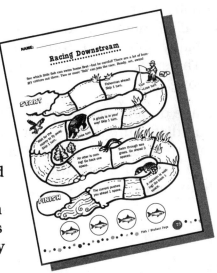

MATERIALS: reproducible page 73, penny, quarters, oaktag, crayons, scissors

Ask your students if they eat fish. Ask them if they can think of other animals that also like to eat fish (Seabirds, seals, otters, bears, and raccoons are just a few. There's even a fishing cat, and a fishing bat!) The game is best played by two to three children. Distribute a copy of page 73 to each student along with a copy of the game rules on this page. Review the instructions with them before they begin. Students will have fun pretending to be fish racing downstream—and at the same time they'll become even more familiar with some of the dangers that real fish encounter. Here's how to play:

1. Ask students to color each fish disk a different color.

2. Then have them cut out the disks and glue them to quarters. Or use quarter-sized pieces of oaktag and mark the disks heads on one side, tails on the other.

3. Students might want to color the game board as well. Once they have, they should cut it out and glue it to a piece of oaktag.

Rules of the Game

1. Flip a penny to see how many spaces you may move.
   Heads=1 Space; Tails=2 Spaces

2. Take turns moving your fish and following the directions on the game board.

3. The first fish to finish wins!

Sizing Up Sharks

MATERIALS: reproducible pages 74 and 75, scissors

When you ask the children what they know about sharks, you will probably come away with images of the great white in *Jaws*. Before they assemble this mini-book, share some of these shark facts with your students:

- There are more than 350 different kinds of sharks.
- They have an excellent sense of smell.
- Sharks don't have smooth scales like most fish, their bodies are covered with scales called "denticles" that have little sharp teeth.
- Many sharks are completely harmless.
- The smallest shark is only about 6 inches long!

Make double sided copies of pages 74 and 75, and distribute them to your students. Have them fold the page lengthwise along the dashed line, and then cut along the solid lines below the sharks to make their books.

BOOK BREAKS

The Rainbow Fish by Marcus Pfister (North-South Books, 1992)

Fish Tales by Nat Segaloff & Paul Erickson (Sterling Publishers, 1990)

Coral Reef Hideaway by Doe Boyle (Smithsonian Institute, 1995)

What Is a Fish? by David Eastman (Troll Association, 1982)

Life in the Sea by Eileen Curran (Troll Association, 1985)

NAME: _____

All About Fish

Can you find the fish below? Circle the animals you think are fish. Use the clues in the center to help you.

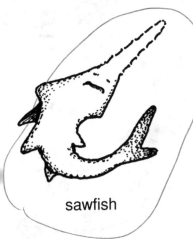

sawfish

dolphin

HOW TO SPOT A FISH

1. **All** fish live in water.
2. **All** fish have backbones.
3. **All** fish breathe through gills.
4. **All** fish are cold-blooded (cannot make their own body heat).
5. **Most** fish have eyes that stay open (because they have no lids).
6. **Most** fish have fins.
7. **Most** fish have scales.
8. **Most** fish lay eggs.

starfish

pirahna

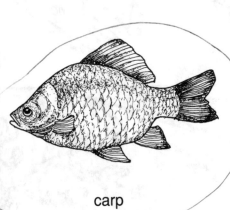

carp

shark

hawksbill

Samuel closed his eyes, made a wish, and WHOOOOOSH!

HE WAS HOME AGAIN!

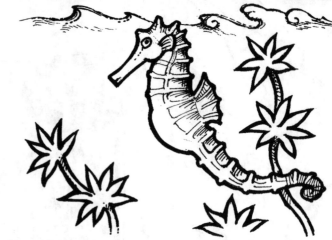

Along swam a starfish, Samuel said sadly, "You don't even twinkle."
"That's true," said the starfish, "but close your eyes, make a wish, . . . and see what happens!"

Along swam a parrotfish.
Samuel waited and waited.
But the parrotfish didn't squawk.

By now, Samuel was VERY hungry, VERY sleepy, and missed his family VERY much!

Samuel was a little seahorse who wanted to see new places.

One day he let the water carry him far, far away from home.

15

After a while, he wrapped his tail around some seagrass. Along swam a cowfish. Samuel waited and waited. But the cowfish didn't moo.

Samuel was getting hungry.

13

Along swam a dogfish. Samuel waited and waited. but the dogfish didn't bark.

Samuel was getting sleepy.

11

Along swam a catfish. Samuel waited and waited. But the catfish didn't meow.

Samuel missed his family.

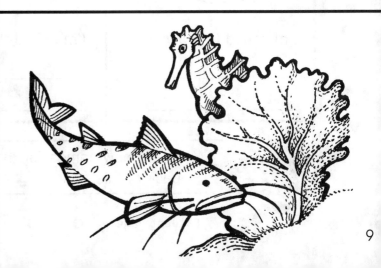

9

NAME: _____

Sea Animal Names

How do you think many sea creatures got their names? These animals have names that tell you something about how they look. Use the word box to find the correct name for each sea creature.

WORD BOX

Sea cucumber
Starfish
Elephant-snout
Spiny urchin
Sawfish
Porcupine puffer

---

1. _____

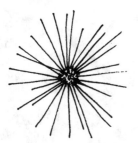

I'm called this because

_____
_____

2. _____

I'm called this because

_____
_____

3. _____

I'm called this because

_____
_____

4. _____

I'm called this because

_____
_____

5. _____

I'm called this because

_____
_____

6. _____

I'm called this because

_____
_____

EXTRA Invent new names for these creatures and write them on the back of this paper.

Pufferfish Puzzle

NAME: _____

ACROSS

1. what fishes swim in
2. a Mako or Great White _____
4. what a fish uses to move through the water
5. what a fish can't close
8. fish use these to balance and steer
10. this fish looks like a snake

DOWN

1. a huge sea-mammal that looks like a fish
2. fish that grizzly bears like to eat
3. a fish that has whiskers is called a _____ fish
6. most fish are covered with these
7. clownfish are found around coral _____
9. a sleek sea-mammal with strong fins and thick fur

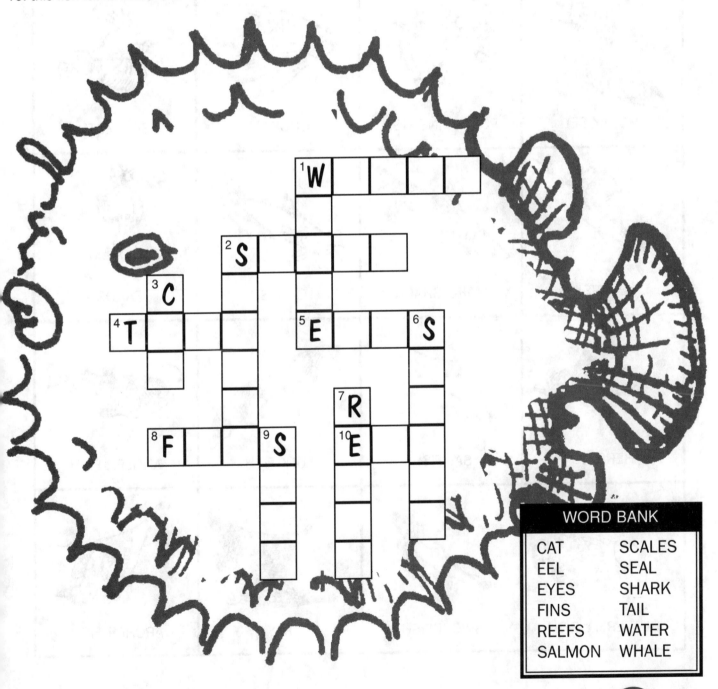

WORD BANK

CAT	SCALES
EEL	SEAL
EYES	SHARK
FINS	TAIL
REEFS	WATER
SALMON	WHALE

Match That Fish!

Do all fish look alike? NO WAY! After you cut these pictures apart you'll have a deck of 16 different kinds of fish. Combine your deck with a classmate's, spread them out picture side down and play "concentration".

MORAY EEL	PORCUPINE FISH	GOURAMI	SEA MOTH
SAILFISH	MAKO SHARK	CATFISH	SEAHORSE
HERRING	SAWFISH	LUNGFISH	ANGLER FISH
BUTTERFLY FISH	SWORDFISH	RAY	ARCHER FISH

Squiggley-Squid
·········

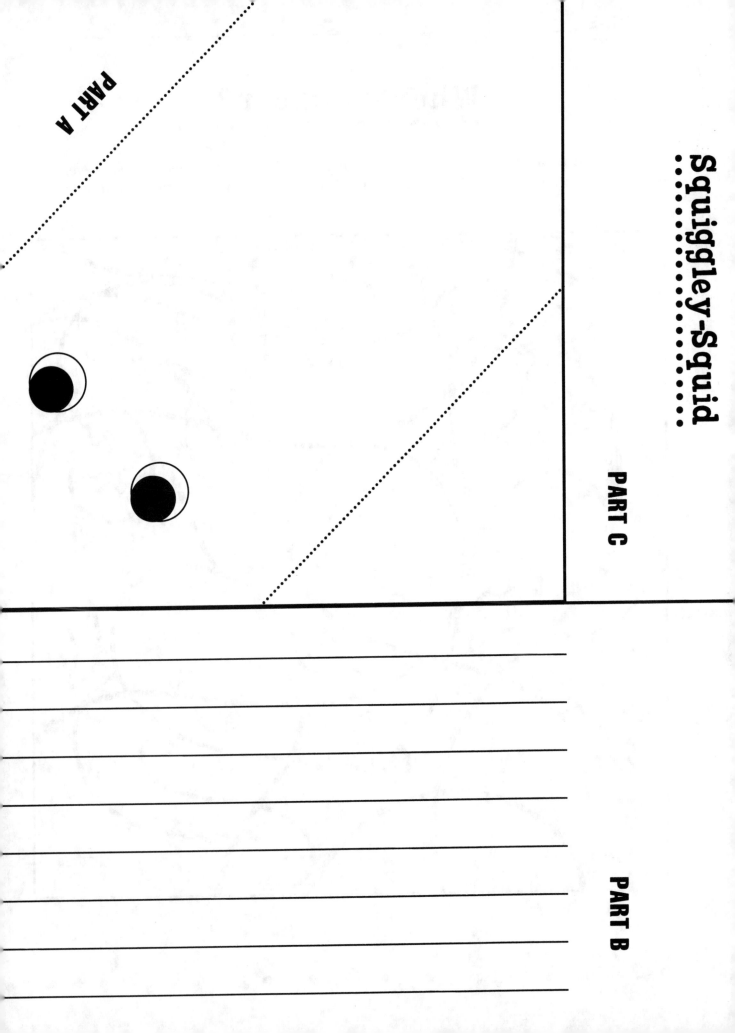

PART A

PART B

PART C

NAME: _____

Where's Oscar?

And what is he? You can solve this mystery by coloring all the spaces with even numbers blue. What's left? Turn this jumbled picture upside down to find out.

NAME: _____

Racing Downstream

See which little fish can swim home first—but be careful! There are a lot of hungry critters out there. Two or more "fish" can join the race. Ready, set, swim!

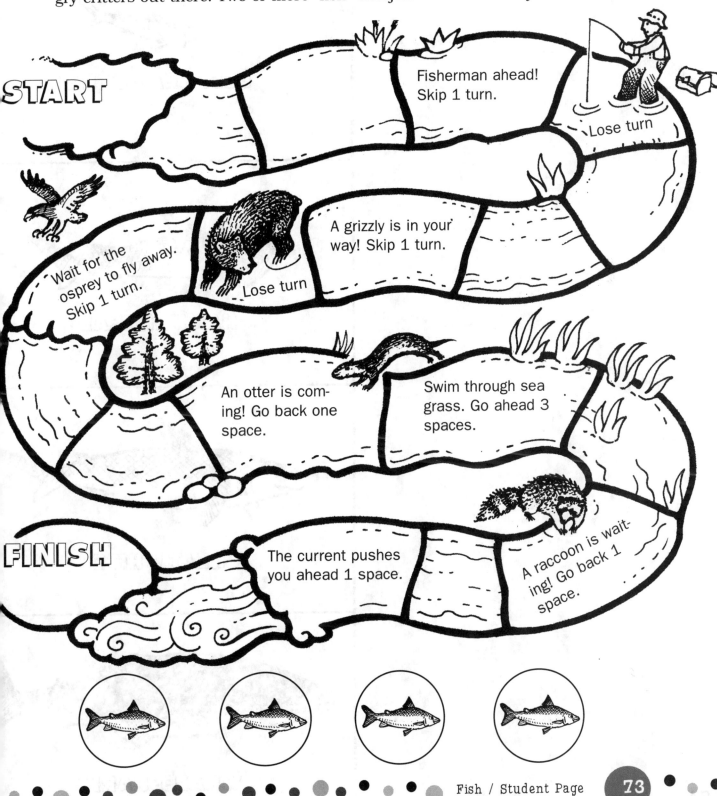

START

Fisherman ahead! Skip 1 turn.

Lose turn

A grizzly is in your way! Skip 1 turn.

Wait for the osprey to fly away. Skip 1 turn.

Lose turn

An otter is coming! Go back one space.

Swim through sea grass. Go ahead 3 spaces.

FINISH

The current pushes you ahead 1 space.

A raccoon is waiting! Go back 1 space.

SIZING UP SHARKS!

Did you know there are more than 350 kinds of sharks? Here are a few—from quite small to super-sized.

DEEPSEA DOGFISH

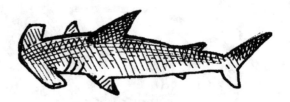

HAMMERHEAD

GREAT WHITE

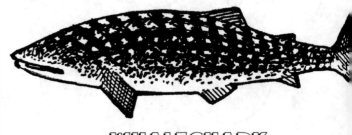

WHALESHARK

This shark is only 12 inches long! It lives deep in the ocean where it's as dark as night. How does it find things? By smell and by making its own light along the sides of its body!

This shark is 18 feet long—That's as long as most living rooms! And look where its eyes are—one on each side of the "hammer". It can't see things in front of its face so it keeps moving its head from side to side.

This is one of the scariest sharks. It's 35 feet long and weights 3 tons—that's as much as a school bus! It never runs out of teeth, either. If a tooth falls out, one of its 20,000 other teeth moves into its place!

This is the largest fish in the world! It can grow to be about 60 feet long, and can weigh more than 2 elephants! But, it's a gentle giant, and divers often "hitch a ride" by holding onto its fins or tail.

Fish Coloring Page

Invite your students to create a new kind of fish by decorating the one below.

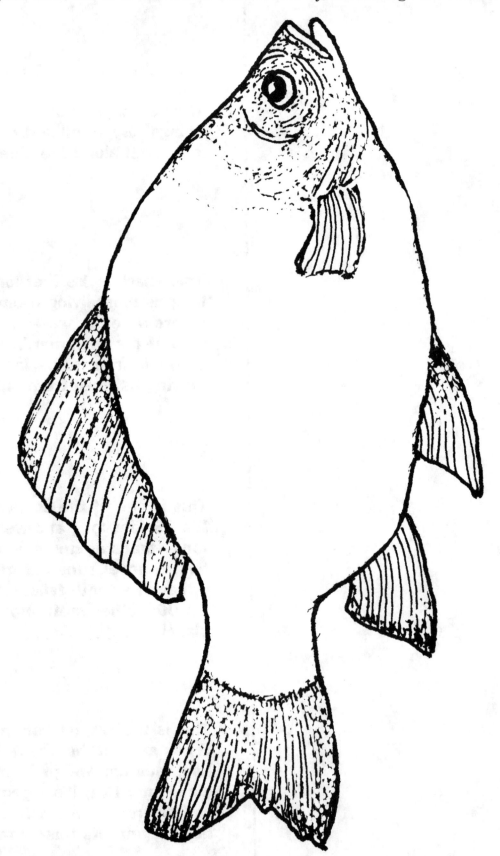

CHAPTER 5

Feathers and Flight
Birds

BACKGROUND INFORMATION

Ask a hundred avid bird-watchers what makes birds so special, and you may get a hundred different answers. It might be the melody of a songbird announcing the arrival of spring, or a cardinal's vivid red flashing against a snowy landscape; it might be the haunting cry of a loon, or the acrobatics of a chickadee. And while the ability to fly is fascinating, it doesn't seem to be the major factor in the appeal of birds. After all, penguins don't fly at all, and few people can observe one without smiling. One ardent bird-watcher (who has seen more than 500 species) claimed it was the variety of bird shapes and behavior that intrigued him the most.

■ And what variety! There are over 8,500 species in colors from drab to day-glo; their tail shapes range from a minimal stump (ant bird) to a thirty-five foot extravaganza (Japanese Phoenix fowl)! And size? From one as small as a moth to one nine feet tall! Even their feet vary: some species have three toes, some have four, and others have feet resembling hooks or paddles. Beak shapes are almost as varied as feather color: from dainty scimitars to kayaks and shoe-horns— each appropriately suited to the bird's diet. Not even flight is standardized: some birds fly in spurts (swifts and swallows), some do a lot of flapping (geese and starlings), some soar, barely moving their wings (hawks and eagles), and others don't fly at all (penguins and ostriches)!

■ Most birds build nests for their eggs and chicks, but there are parasitic birds who deposit their eggs (one at a time) into the nests of unsuspecting "host" species. Some nests, like the bee hummingbird's, are as tiny as hazelnuts, while others, like those of the mound bird, are heaps of soil and plant debris as large as a living room! Tailorbirds raise their young in leaves they've sewn together with spider silk, and swallows build nests of mud. But emperor penguins, breeding in plantless Antarctica, incubate their eggs on the tops of their feet!

■ So what do these scaly-legged warm blooded vertebrates have in common? They all lay eggs, and they all have feathers!

■ As your students complete the following activities, they'll find out about feathers, nests, and feet, and learn to tell what a bird eats just by looking at its beak. They'll also get to meet a group of birds that are special because they don't fly!

STUDENT ACTIVITIES

All About Birds

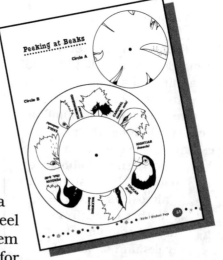

MATERIALS: reproducible page 84, pencil

When students are asked to name something that makes birds special, flight is usually their first response. Try it with your class. Remind the children that other things fly, too: all bats, most insects, and other creatures that seem to fly (they actually glide) like flying geckos, flying fish, and flying squirrels. (Ask why they aren't birds.) There are birds that don't fly at all, but are still birds. After you give copies of this reference sheet to your students, discuss the characteristics. While other animals may meet *some* of the criteria, only birds meet them *all*—and easiest for the children to remember—they're the only animal with feathers.

When students are sure of the characteristics, ask them to circle the birds on the page. **Answers:** *falcon, macaw, penguin, pintail duck, toucan*

Peeking at Beaks

MATERIALS: reproducible page 85, scissors, brass fastener

Explain that most birds prefer specific foods, and that their beaks are clear indications of their diets. To make the wheels, have students cut out both circles and make a small hole in the center of each. Then ask them to put circle A on top of circle B. They should secure the two with a brass fastener. After they assemble the wheel and match each bird with its beak, ask them if they think the beaks are the best shape for the foods the birds eat. Could it be improved? What would happen if a toucan tried to catch an insect? Could a hummingbird catch a mouse? Could a nightjar sip nectar?

What Neat Feet!

MATERIALS: reproducible page 86, scissors, paste

Make copies of page 86 and distribute them to your students. They'll discover that birds' feet are almost as varied as their beaks! The clues will help them match each pair of feet to their rightful owner.
Answers: *sparrow-2, penguin-5, sandpiper-4, eagle-3, duck-1*

Finding Out About Feathers

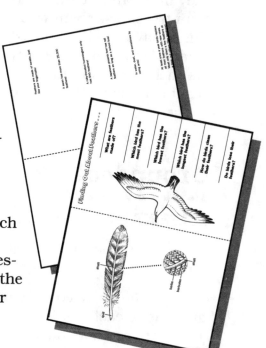

MATERIALS: reproducible pages 87 and 88, scissors

Other kinds of animals may fly, and others may lay eggs, but only birds have feathers. Their structure and texture seem to intrigue children, and just finding a stray feather delights them. This simple mini-book is designed to answer some frequently asked questions about feathers.

Make a double-sided copy of pages 87 and 88 for each of your students. Have them fold the page along the dashed line, then cut along the solid lines. Each question is answered behind its corresponding flap, and the back of the mini-book has an illustration of a feather and its construction.

Which Nest Is Best?

MATERIALS: reproducible page 89, pencil

Explain to your students that nests fulfill a very specific purpose: they provide a safe place for birds to lay eggs and they also serve as a nursery in which to raise offspring until they are self-sufficient. As students identify which nest belongs to which bird, they will come to understand how a bird's size and environment influence the kind of nest it builds. **Answers:** *1. C, 2. D, 3. B, 4. A*

Birder's Treasure Hunt

MATERIALS: reproducible page 90, pencil

This would be a perfect springtime activity for the whole class. You may want to take your class to a nearby park for the treasure hunt, and possibly have a picnic as well. Depending on your class they can hunt individually, in pairs, or in small groups. You might even want to have the whole class hunt together. Discuss their findings. If they find berries, ask them what kind they think they are. If they find a nest (caution them not to remove nests from trees), ask them what kind of bird they think may have built it. Ask what they think the caterpillar will become. If they find stray feathers, help them speculate on the kind of bird that lost it. What color is it? What kinds of birds are in the area?

Grounded!

MATERIALS: pages 91 and 92, scissors

Here are the nonconformists, the rule-breakers: birds that don't fly!

Make a double-sided copy of this mini-book and give one to each student.
To make the book, have the children fold along the dashed vertical line, and then again along the horizontal dashed line, with the title face up. Then ask them to open the book and cut along the solid lines which will form flaps.

EXTRA: After the children have a chance to read about the birds, challenge them to find their homes on a map or globe.

Birds of the Rainbow

MATERIALS: reproducible page 93, crayons

Here are three rainbow-hued birds for your students to color. One, appropriately is called the rainbow lorikeet. Give each student two copies of the sheet. Ask them to color the birds on the first sheet according to the color key. Then let them create a whole new look for the birds on the second copy, and give them descriptive names of their own.

Penguin Puppet Pals

MATERIALS: reproducible page 94, cardboard, a craft stick, glue, scissors, markers or crayons, tape

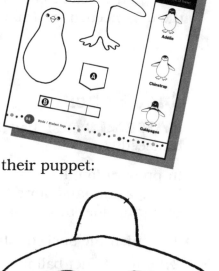

Your students can make a puppet that will waddle and waggle. Distribute a copy of reproducible page 94 to each student along with the necessary art supplies. Explain to students that there are 18 different kinds of penguins, each with a look of its own.

Have students decide which kind of penguin they would like to make—an Adélie, a Galápagos, or a Chinstrap. Once they have chosen one of the above penguins, have them follow these simple steps to make their puppet:

1. Glue a copy of reproducible page 94 to a piece of cardboard.
2. Color the penguin and then cut out each part along the solid lines.
3. Place the penguin face down. And glue the flipper/feet piece to the penguin's body so that the feet are just a little bit lower than the body.
4. Then tape part A down on both sides as shown.
5. Fold part B on the dotted lines and tape it to the flipper section as shown to form a tab.

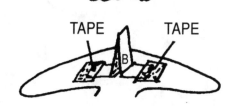

6. Attach the craft stick to part A with three pieces of tape.

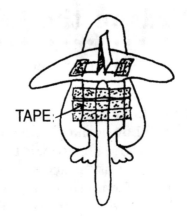

TAPE

Once students have assembled their puppets, all they have to do is move the tab from side to side to see the penguin move its feet and flippers.

Have students point out the defining characteristics of their penguin (the adelie has white rings around its eyes; the chinstrap has a thin black line under its chin; the Galapagos has two stripes on its chest). Ask students to think of a nickname for their penguins based on these characteristics.

Fast-Food Fly-Ins

What better way to see birds than to offer them tempting food? These easy feeding stations offer birds what they need most in winter: protein and fat. The children can make them in class, take them home to hang outside, refill them as needed, and have a grand opportunity to see many local birds.

Suet Snack

MATERIALS: mesh bag (from onions or other vegetables), string, suet, birdseed

In preparation, have your students ask an adult to melt beef fat in a pan, pour it into a can, and store it in the freezer to create the suet. Once it is time to bring the suet to school, have the students do the following:

1. Squish the suet (the frozen fat) in their hands to form a ball.
2. Roll the suet ball into birdseed.
3. Put the suet ball into the mesh bag and hang it from a branch with a piece of string

Peanut Butter Pine Cone

MATERIALS: pine cone, craft stick, peanut butter, eye screw, birdseed, string

1. Help students press and turn an eye-screw into the top of their pine cone. Make sure it "grabs" hold.

2. Then have them use a craft stick or their fingers to stuff peanut butter into all the spaces of their pine cone.

3. Next, have students roll their pine cone in some birdseed.

4. Finally, they should tie one end of the string through the eye of the screw, and the other to a tree branch.

Tell your students they'll need a little patience. It may take several days before the birds discover these mini-restaurants. But once they do, the bird traffic might get very heavy!

BOOK BREAKS

Baby Birds and How They Grow by Jane R. McCavley (National Geographic, 1983)

Eagles by John Bennett Wexo (Creative Editions, 1989)

Penguins by Robin Bernard (Scholastic, 1995)

When Birds Change Their Feathers by Roma Gans (Crowell, 1980)

A Year of Birds by Ashly Wolff (Dodd, Mead, 1984)

All About Birds

Can you find the birds below? Circle the animals you think are birds. Use the clues in the center to help you.

macaw

trogon

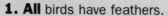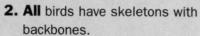

HOW TO SPOT A BIRD

1. **All** birds have feathers.
2. **All** birds have skeletons with backbones.
3. **All** birds have lungs and breathe air.
4. **All** birds are warm-blooded.
5. **All** baby birds hatch from eggs.
6. **Most** birds can fly.
7. **Most** birds build nests for their eggs.
8. **Most** birds feed their newly hatched chicks.

bat

giant moth

pintail duck

toucan

penguin

Peeking at Beaks

Circle A

Circle B

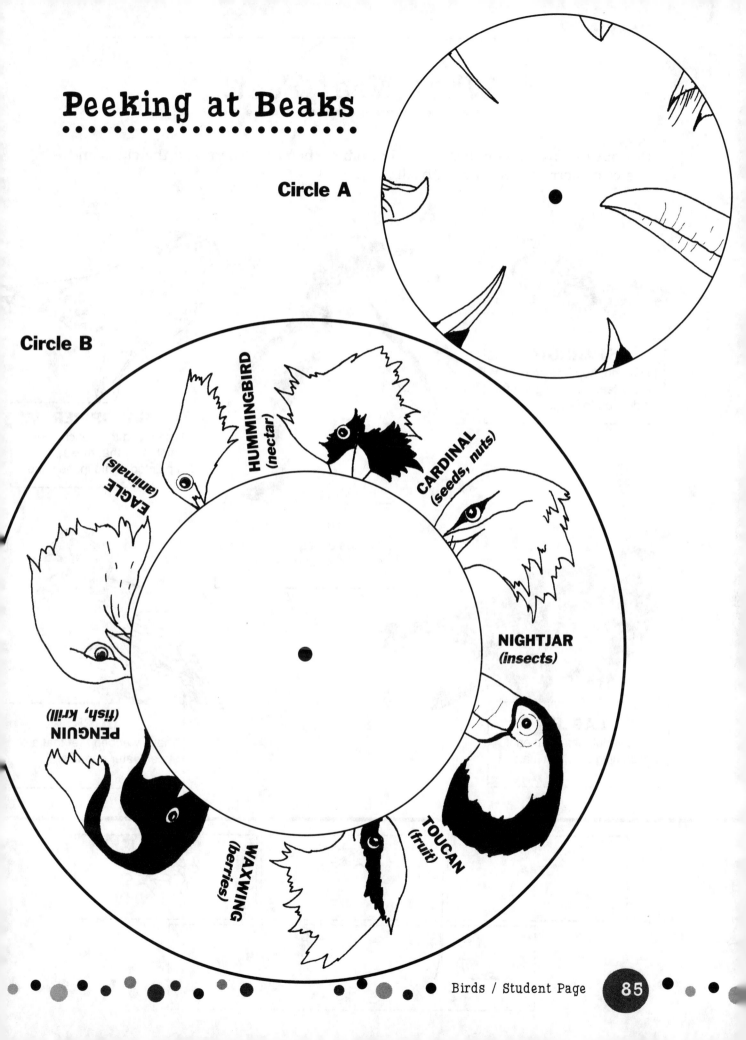

HUMMINGBIRD *(nectar)*

CARDINAL *(seeds, nuts)*

EAGLE *(animals)*

NIGHTJAR *(insects)*

PENGUIN *(fish, krill)*

WAXWING *(berries)*

TOUCAN *(fruit)*

What Neat Feet!

Cut out the five pairs of feet at the bottom of the page. Then read the clues and paste the correct feet on each bird!

SPARROW
I can hop, hop hop on my skinny feet. They're good for holding on to branches, too.

SANDPIPER
I run along the beach on dainty feet that make 3-pointed prints in the sand.

PENGUIN
My wide strong feet keep me from slipping on the ice.

EAGLE
My powerful feet are meant for catching small animals.

DUCK
I have webbed feet that are super water paddles.

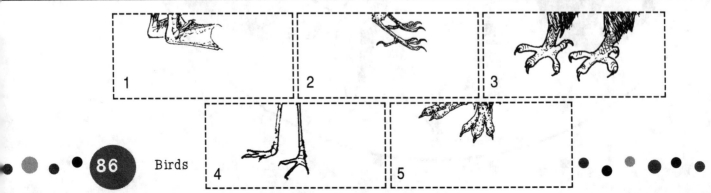

1

2

3

4

5

Finding Out About Feathers . . .

What are feathers made of?

Which bird has the most feathers?

Which bird has the fewest feathers?

Which bird has the longest feathers?

How do birds clean their feathers?

Do birds lose their feathers?

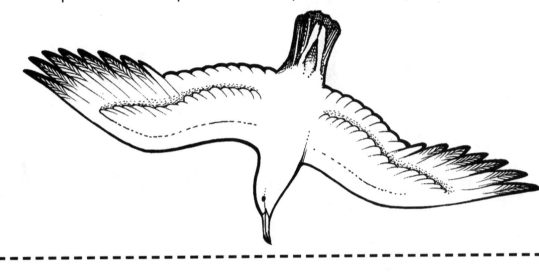

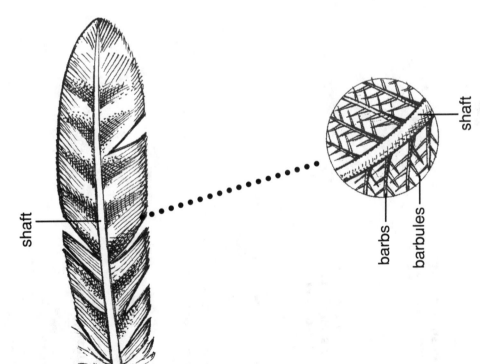

shaft

quill

barbs

barbules

shaft

Feathers are made of keratin, just like your fingernails!

A swan has more than 25,000 feathers!

A ruby-throated hummingbird only has 940 feathers.

A Japanese phoenix fowl has tail feathers as long as a school bus!

In water, dust, and sometimes by using ants!

At least once a year birds replace all their feathers with new ones. Most only shed a few feathers at a time, but others (like penguins) do it all at once!

Which Nest Is Best?

Read the clues to discover which bird built which nest and draw a line connecting the bird with its nest.

1. Weaver Bird

Can you guess how I make my nest, my name gives it away. Plus, my nest looks a lot like a basket made of grass and vines. The only difference is that the opening is on the bottom, not the top.

A.

2. Humming Bird

My nest is super small! I make it by carefully weaving together moss, dried weeds, leaves, seeds, and spider webs. I line it with feathers for extra warmth.

B.

3. Barn Swallow

If you look in a tree you won't see me! And unlike other birds, my nest is bumpy and hard. That's because I make it out of mud!

C.

4. Robin

I may not be big, but I still need my nest of mud and straw to be very strong. That's because it protects my babies while I am away looking for food.

D.

Birder's Treasure Hunt

Here are a bunch of things that are part of a bird's life. See how many you can find. Put a check by the things you think a bird might eat.

feather	**seeds**	**nest**
cricket	**acorns**	**worm**
spider silk	**berries**	**caterpillar**
butterfly	**beetle**	**woodpecker hole**

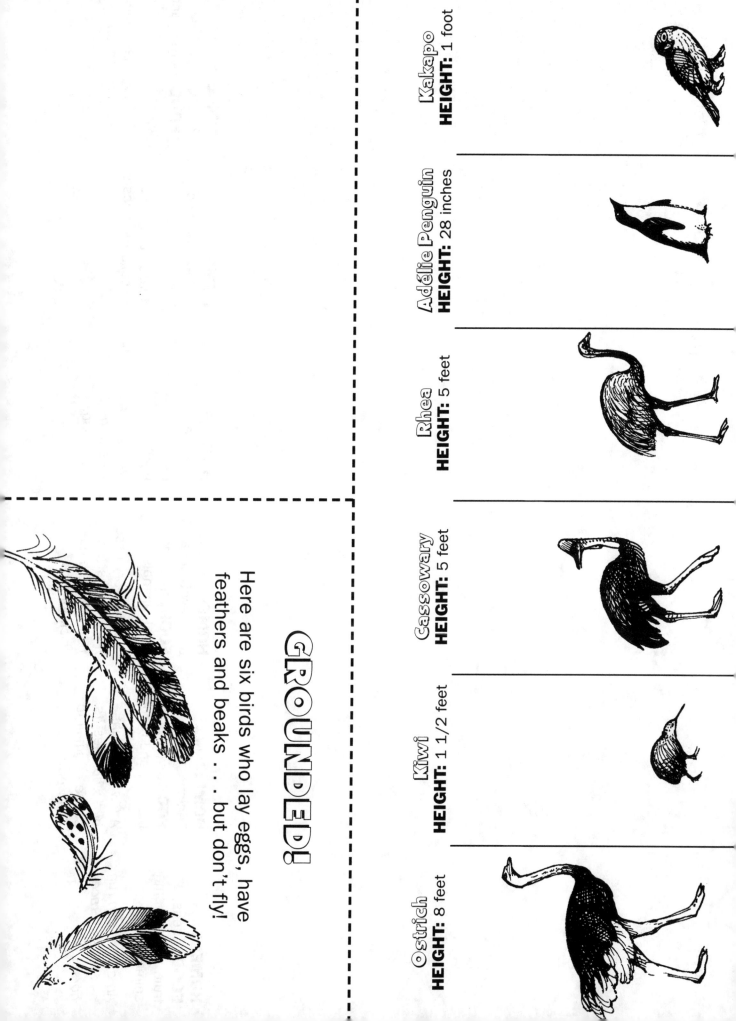

GROUNDED!

Here are six birds who lay eggs, have feathers and beaks . . . but don't fly!

Kakapo
HEIGHT: 1 foot

Adélie Penguin
HEIGHT: 28 inches

Rhea
HEIGHT: 5 feet

Cassowary
HEIGHT: 5 feet

Kiwi
HEIGHT: 1 1/2 feet

Ostrich
HEIGHT: 8 feet

HOME: Africa
FOOD: seeds, fruit, insects, small animals

An ostrich can run as fast as a race-horse!

HOME: New Zealand
FOOD: worms, insects, and berries

A kiwi is a night bird who uses its sense of smell to find worms.

HOME: Australia and New Guinea
FOOD: fruit and small animals

A cassowary uses its "hard hat" to push through the thick forest.

HOME: South America
FOOD: insects and plants

Rheas swallow pebbles to help digest their food.

HOME: Antarctica
FOOD: fish and krill

Adélies use pebbles to build their nests.

HOME: New Zealand
FOOD: berries and ferns

This shy night parrot is an endangered species.

Birds of the Rainbow

There are birds with red feathers, and birds with blue, yellow, or green feathers.
But there are some birds that have almost as many colors as a box of crayons!
Use your crayons according to the color key box to color their feathers.

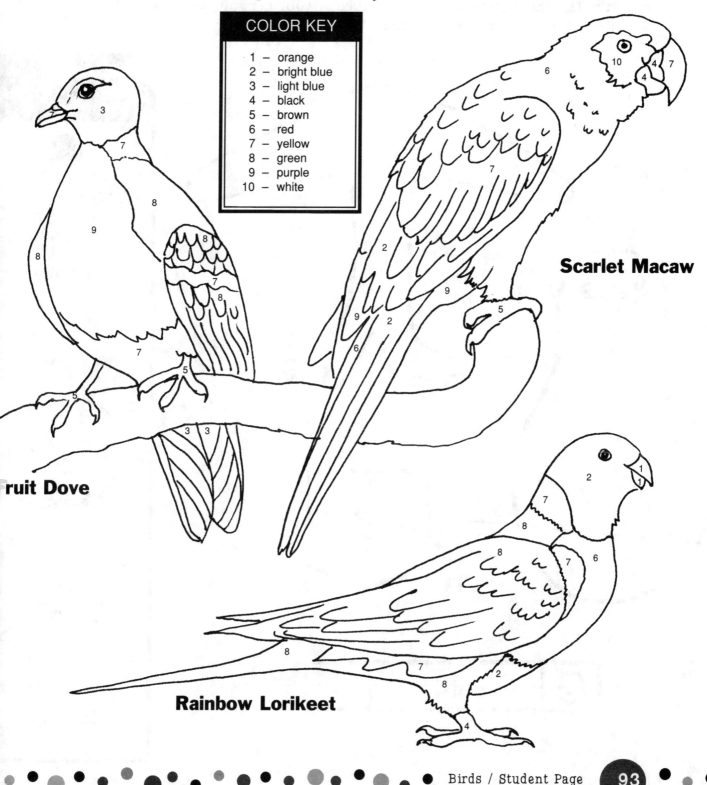

COLOR KEY

1 – orange
2 – bright blue
3 – light blue
4 – black
5 – brown
6 – red
7 – yellow
8 – green
9 – purple
10 – white

Scarlet Macaw

Fruit Dove

Rainbow Lorikeet

Popsicle Pal Puppet

You can make a puppet that will waddle and waggle. Look at the pictures below and decide if you want your puppet to be an Adélie, a Chinstrap, or a Galápagos penguin. Use the picture as a guide and color your penguin so it looks like your favorite one. Don't forget to color the edges of the wings!

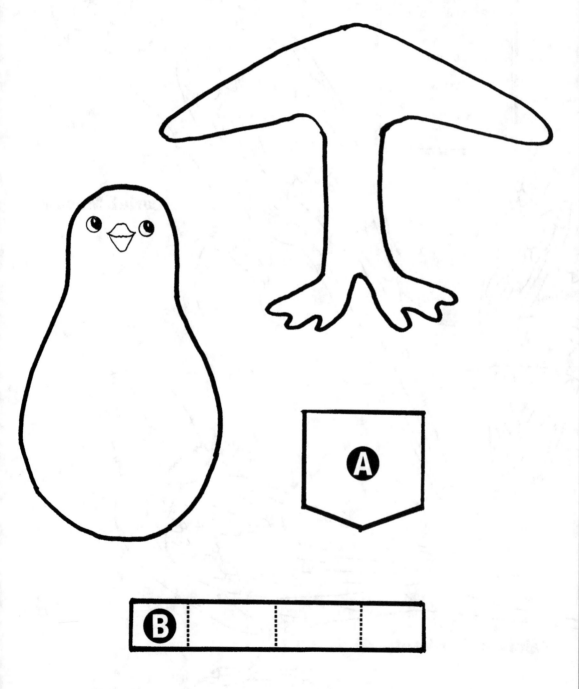

Make your penguin look like one of the

Adélie

Chinstrap

Galápagos

CHAPTER 6

All Together Now
The Animal Kingdom.

BACKGROUND INFORMATION

Now that you've looked at characteristics that distinguish each animal class, let's consider the many things they have in common. Whether they are furred or feathered, have scales or plates, or occupy different ecological niches and different links on the food chain, animals still share similarities. For instance, can you imagine what a honey bee has in common with a whooping crane? Both use "dance" to communicate. Members of all animal classes lay eggs: insects, reptiles, fish, birds, amphibians, and even three mammals (the platypus and two kinds of spiny anteaters)! And camouflage? There are masters of that game in all classes: the polar bear (mammal), the peppered moth (insect), the desert adder (reptile), the bittern (bird), the glass frog (amphibian), and the stonefish (fish)—to name a few.

Physical and behavioral traits are geared to benefit the particular species, whether it's an acute sense of hearing, scent marking, armor plating, or producing vast numbers of young. Survival mechanisms are repeated throughout the entire animal kingdom from grasshoppers to gorillas. Consider these similarities:

PARENTAL CARE:
Although mammals and birds are known to lavish attention on their offspring, many insects—particularly the social ones like bees, ants, and termites— also care for their young. So do cichlids (fish), alligators (reptiles), and forest toads (amphibians).

BUILDING:
Birds aren't the only builders. Termites, bees, and spiders are pretty impressive architects as are beavers and prairie dogs.

TOOL USING:
Chimps whittle twigs to probe insect nests. A sea otter will dive for a flat stone, flip over on its back and lay the stone on its chest. Then it smashes mollusks open by battering them against the stone.

Ornithologists have discovered more than 30 bird species that use tools. Many species use stones as anvils, but there are other tool-users, too: tailorbirds make nests by stitching leaves together with knotted fiber; woodpecker finches use cactus spines to poke into insect holes; bowerbirds paint their constructions with "brushes" they shape from wood, and "paint" they make by combining fruit juice with their saliva!

CHEMICAL DEFENSE:
This mechanism is used by stinging insects like wasps and bees. Of the amphibians, the most famous chemical warriors are the poison arrow frogs, but even common toads have mildly poisonous skin. Some mammals, like moles and certain shrews have venomous salivary glands, and we all know how skunks use a chemical defense! Many reptiles, like mambas, boomslangs, and kraits, have highly toxic venom, and so do stonefish and box jellyfish. There are even some tropical birds that have poisonous flesh and feathers!

MIGRATION: Who's on the move? Whales, caribou, fur seals, salmon, swallows, sea turtles, penguins, spiny lobsters, and monarch butterflies all make seasonal trips to mate, spawn, or follow food. But Arctic terns have no rivals. Every year they fly from the Arctic to the Antarctic and back again—that's more than 25,000 miles!

HIBERNATION: Winter is a hard time for wildlife, and different mechanisms have evolved to deal with it. Some animals migrate to warmer climates; some prepare for the scarcity of food by stashing away a larder while food is still plentiful; some grow a heavy layer of fat and fur and simply get through it. But others find a snug place, slow their metabolisms to a torpor, and sleep away the cold months. Ground squirrels and marmots living in the coldest regions may sleep as long as six or seven months! Several kinds of bats and bears hibernate, too. Scientists recently discovered that certain hummingbirds, swifts, and whippoorwills also hibernate. Many insects, reptiles, amphibians—all ectothermic (cold-blooded)—also survive the winter by hibernating under bark, leaf mulch, or deep in the mud.

ARMOR AND SPINES: Shellfish and turtles, snails, armadillos, pangolins, and even rhinos, are protected by hard coverings. There's even a bird, the flightless cassowary, who wears a "hard hat" to protect its head in the underbrush. Other animals such as porcupines, hedgehogs, armadillo lizards, porcupine fish, and sea urchins possess sharp spines, quills, or needles.

SOCIAL GROUPS: Some animals are loners who need no help surviving on their own. But some benefit from safety in numbers, with more eyes on the alert for danger. Predators, like lions and wolves, form groups because they have greater success in hunting. Social insects, like ants, termites, and bees, have specific roles within complex societies. Cooperative living benefits all kinds of herds, packs, pods, flocks, schools, troops, prides, and swarms.

FLIGHT: If we broaden the word "flight" to include gliding, we can find airborne creatures beyond insects, birds, and bats. Among reptiles there are both snakes and lizards that can sail 200 feet on flaps of skin. Flying frogs glide from branch to branch using mini-parachutes of skin stretched between their toes. Flying fish have large pectoral fins that allow them to leap 15 feet out of the water and "sail" in the air for hundreds of feet.

STUDENT ACTIVITIES

Animal Kingdom Dominoes

MATERIALS: reproducible pages 101 and 102, oaktag, scissors, paste

Make a copy of pages 101 and 102 for each child and ask them to paste the sheets to oaktag. As students cut out the dominoes, review the five animal categories with them. (Although each student will make a complete set of 36 dominoes, they'll only need one set per pair of students to play the game.)

Here's how to play:

1. The game begins with all dominoes turned face down. Each player picks and keeps 4 dominoes, but doesn't show them to her or his opponent.

2. Have students decide on the matching criteria (i.e., mammal to mammal; predator to predator; amphibian to amphibian, etc.) before they begin playing.

3. Spin a pencil or toss a coin to see who goes first. Player A lays a domino face up on the table.

4. Player B must be able to match the determined criteria in order to put a domino down. If Player B can't do that, he or she must draw from the pile until picking a domino that can be played.

5. Players alternate turns, and whoever gets rid of all his or her dominoes first is the winner. If, at the end, neither player can play their remaining dominoes, the one with the fewest is the winner.

EXTENSION: Make extra sets of the dominoes for each student. Have them cut the dominoes in half and then sort the 36 animals using different criteria:

land-dwelling/water-dwelling
carnivore/herbivore/omnivore
warm-blooded/cold-blooded

Venn Diagrams

To help your students understand that different kinds of animals share similar traits, draw a group of Venn diagrams on the board. Enlist students' help to determine the factors. Start with a two ring Venn—like WARM-BLOODED, either setting the criteria first, or overlapping a BIRD ring with a MAMMAL ring—and seeing what the kids come up with as a common factor. Work up to three and four ring Venns.

Staying Safe

MATERIALS: reproducible page 103, pencil

Ask the students to think of ways animals stay safe from predators. List them on the board: CAMOU-FLAGE, ARMOR, CHEMICALS, SPIKES, SPEED. Offer them some examples of chemicals (poison, strong smelling spray, irritant, etc.), armor (thick hard covering), and spikes (sharp needle-like things that are part of an animal's covering). Distribute copies of page 103 and challenge students to figure out what each animal uses to stay safe.

Confusing Cousins

MATERIALS: reproducible pages 104 and 105

It's very hard to tell some animals apart, even for adults. But it's a lot of fun to be able to tell just who's who, and quite easy if you know what to look for. Make enough double-sided copies of pages 104 and 105 for all your students. Then have them follow these simple steps to assemble their mini-books.

1. Put the paper title-side down. Fold the bottom third up to the dotted line so that the tortoise/turtle section and monkey/ape sections show.

2. Fold the top third down so only the cheetah/leopard section shows.

3. Fold inward along the dashed lines. First flatten the right side, then bring the left side over it. now the title page should be in front.

4. Open each triple section at a time, read the clues to find out who is who and write the animal's name beneath the picture.

Discuss each of the "pairs," and see if the children can pick out other helpful characteristics to tell them apart. (You might hint: How do the rabbit's ear differ from the hare's? How about the shapes of their bodies, are they different?) Challenge the students to name other confusing cousins and to find ways to tell them apart. Some ideas:

seal/sea lions	**moose/elk**	**duck/goose**	**alligator/crocodile**
llama/alpaca	**fox/coyote**	**starling/crow**	**butterfly/moth**

Snoozers
• • • • • • • • •

MATERIALS: reproducible pages 106 and 107, glue, scissors

Make copies of both pages and give each child a set. To form flaps, have them cut along the dotted lines on the title page. Then have them place the title page on top of the second page and glue the pages together along the edges. As they lift each flap, a different winter sleepyhead is revealed.

Forest Friends
• • • • • • • • • • • • • •

MATERIALS: reproducible page 108, crayons, scissors, sticky tape, glue, oaktag

Here is a group of forest animal finger puppets. Have the children paste the page to oaktag, color the animals, and cut them out. Show them how to fit the puppets to their fingers using sticky tape to hold the ring together. They can use the puppets as characters in *The Tortoise and the Hare* (pages 109 and 110), or act out their own stories and plays.

The Tortoise and the Hare

MATERIALS: reproducible pages 109 and 110, finger puppets

Your students will have fun acting out this version of an old Aesop fable. To make it special, the students can prepare a "set" by painting forest scenes on a long stretch of newsprint (from a roll). Make sure they include the forest clearing at one end and the finish line and pond at the other.

The Biggest and the Best

MATERIALS: reproducible page 111 and 112, scissors, oaktag, glue

Who is the tallest? Who's the biggest? Who's the fastest? Your students will learn about some super animals by making these cards. Distribute copies of pages 111 and 112 to each student and help them follow these directions.

1. Paste the pages to oaktag for added durability.
2. Once the glue has dried, cut the cards apart along the solid lines.
3. Then fold each card in half along the dotted line and paste the sides together.

Once students have made their cards they can use them to quiz each other, they can invent their own card games, or they can use them in any other way you see fit.

Animal Kingdom Dominoes

alpaca — mammal	antbird — bird	badger — mammal
fish — carp	mammal — goatimundi	mammal — ferret
gallinule — bird	black vulture — bird	spadefish — fish
bird — tyrant flycatcher	reptile — banded gecko	bird — hoatzin
jackrabbit — mammal	harpy eagle — bird	jerboa — mammal
mammal — loris	mammal — lemur	reptile — horned lizard

Animal Kingdom Dominoes

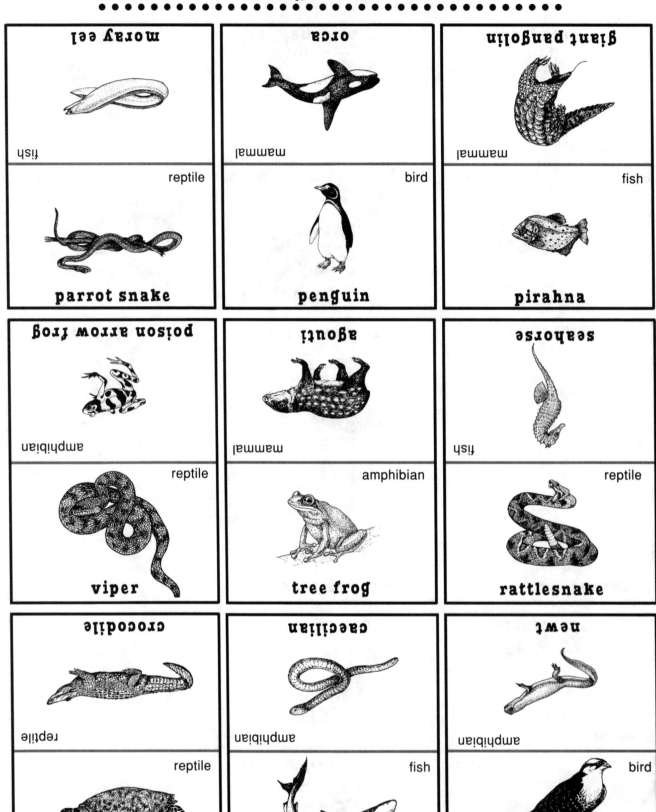

moray eel	orca	giant pangolin
fish	mammal	mammal
reptile	bird	fish
parrot snake	penguin	pirahna
poison arrow frog	agouti	seahorse
amphibian	mammal	fish
reptile	amphibian	reptile
viper	tree frog	rattlesnake
crocodile	caecilian	newt
reptile	amphibian	amphibian
reptile	fish	bird
hawksbill	shark	falcon

NAME: _____

Staying Safe

Can you tell how these animals protect themselves?

kangaroo ◯

armadillo ◯

hare ◯

Here are five different things that help protect animals:

1. camouflage
2. armor
3. chemicals
4. spikes
5. speed

Look at each animal picture carefully and decide which way it protects itself. Write the number in the circle.

skunk ◯

turtle ◯

porcupine ◯

chameleon ◯

walking leaf ◯

thorny devil ◯

rattlesnake ◯

Cheetah or Leopard?

Are you seeing spots? A leopard's spots look a lot like flowers. A cheetah's spots look like little black eggs.

Confusing Cousins

Some animals make us wonder WHICH is WHICH and WHO is WHO! Knowing what to look for will help you find out. Read the clues, and then write the name of each animal under its picture.

Tortoise or Turtle?

Watch those feet! A turtle is in water a lot, so its toes are webbed. Sometimes they're flippers! A tortoise lives on land and its toes are separate.

Monkey or Ape?

Tails can be tattle-tales!
Some monkeys use their tails
like an extra arm. But an ape
doesn't have any tail at all!

Rabbit or Hare?

Check out the legs! A rabbit
can scamper into a burrow,
but a hare, who lives on open
fields, needs long legs to run
fast and far.

Frog or Toad?

Look at the skin! A frog has
much smoother skin than its
lumpy, bumpy relative!

Snoozers

· · · · · · · · · · · · · ·

Have you ever wondered how animals manage to survive the winter? In cold areas with lots of snow, food becomes hard to find. Some animals can travel to warmer places; others eat food they've stored for the cold season. But some creatures find cozy places, close their eyes, and snooze until the weather turns warm again!

Cut along the dotted lines, then lift the flaps to see who's snoozing where—but *sshhh*, don't wake them!

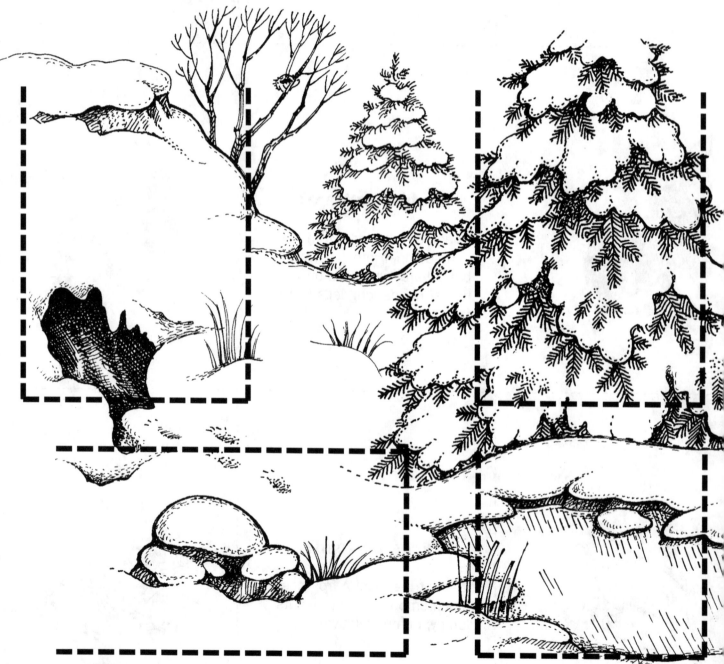

Wrapped in their wings, **bats** sleep upside down. They'll stay in the cave until the weather is warm and bugs are flying around again.

The little **dormouse** makes a special winter nest of leaves and soft moss. Then it curls in a tight ball and snoozes through the whole winter.

When the air gets nippy, the **woodchuck** heads for deep snug tunnels in the woods. It may sleep for half a year.

As soon as the first ice forms on the edge of a pond, the **frog** buries itself in the leaves and mud at the bottom.

Forest Friends

The Tortoise and the Hare

A Play Based on an Aesop Fable

Cast (In Order of Appearance)
Narrator
Francis Fox
Sammy Skunk
Simon Squirrel
Ricky Raccoon
Homer Hare
Thomas Tortoise

NARRATOR: Very early in the morning on a lovely spring day, a group of animals gathered in a forest clearing. They were trying to decide how to spend the day.

FRANCIS FOX: How about playing hide-and-seek? (*There is a chorus of no*)

SAMMY SKUNK: I know. . . we could play catch with acorns (*There is a chorus of no*)

SIMON SQUIRREL: Anybody want to play hopscotch? (*There is a chorus of no*)

RICKY RACCOON: So what *will* we do today?

HOMER HARE: I know! Let's race from the big oak tree to the pond. That's only three miles!

FRANCIS FOX: I don't want to race you, Homer. You always win!

SIMON SQUIRREL: Me neither . . .

RICKY RACCOON: Are you kidding, Homer? I'd only race you up a tree.

HOMER HARE: How about you, Sammy? Will you race me to the pond?

SAMMY SKUNK: No way, Homer . . .

NARRATOR: Suddenly a quiet voice was heard.

THOMAS TORTOISE: (*Very quietly*) I'll race you.

NARRATOR: The animals turned toward Thomas Tortoise not believing what they had heard. (*All animals act confused "Huh?" "What did you say?"*)

THOMAS TORTOISE: I said I'll race you, Homer.

(*The others are surprised at first and then try to hide their giggles. Finally all the animals move to the big oak tree. Simon Squirrel scratches a starting line in the dirt and Thomas and Homer take their places behind it.*)

SIMON SQUIRREL: On your mark. get ready . . .get set . . .GO!

(*Homer takes off and is out of sight almost immediately. Thomas has only taken a few slow steps.*)

NARRATOR: Much later in the afternoon, there is nobody in sight except for Homer. He's snoozing against a birch tree, just six feet from the finish line at the pond. His eyes are closed and he is gently snoring. Then Sammy Skunk, Simon Squirrel, Ricky Raccoon, and Francis Fox appear.

(*The four animals walk up to the sleeping hare.*)

SAMMY SKUNK: Some race this is! One racer is slow as molasses and the other is snoring!

HOMER HARE: (*Opening one eye.*) Shhh! Can't you see I am trying to get a little shut-eye, Ricky? Besides, Thomas won't be here for hours! (*He closes his eye and goes back to sleep.*)

SIMON SQUIRREL: I can see Thomas coming down the road. What do you guys think, should we let Homer know?

HOMER HARE: (*Opens one eye and looks down the road.*) Shhh! Be quiet, you guys! I see Thomas, but he won't be here for another forty minutes and I only need five seconds to cross the finish line. (*He goes back to sleep.*)

(*Sammy Skunk, Ricky Raccoon, Simon Squirrel, and Francis Fox all watch Thomas plod across the finish line. They pat his shell, and jump up and down cheering his victory. All the excitement wakes Homer who jumps to his feet.*)

FRANCIS FOX: Good thing you woke up, Homer! You don't want to miss the big party we're having for Thomas! He just won the race!!!

THE END

The Biggest and the Best

Which is the longest snake?

What is the largest sea-mammal?

What's the tallest bird?

Python. Imagine a yard stick, now imagine 11 of them in a row. That would equal 33 feet, that's how long a python can grow!

The Blue Whale. It can be 100 feet long. That's even longer than two railroad cars!

The Ostrich. It can grow to be 9 feet tall. That is taller than the tallest basketball player!

What bird can fly the fastest?

What's the largest frog?

What's the largest insect?

The White-Throated Swift. It can fly 110 mph. That is much faster than the average motorcar can travel!

The Goliath Frog. It is 16 inches long! That's as long as a computer keyboard.

An Indonesian Stick Insect. It is twelve inches long. That's as long as the average ruler!

What mammal jumps the farthest?

The Red Kangaroo. It can cover 35 feet in one hop! That's about as long as a school bus!

What waterbird dives the deepest?

The Emperor Penguin. It can dive nearly 900 feet deep. That is as deep as 8 football fields!

What's the largest land mammal?

The African Elephant. It weighs as much as 5 cars and it is taller than a basketball hoop!

What mammal runs the fastest?

The Cheetah. It can reach speeds of 60 mph. That is faster than the highway speed limit in most states!

What bird flies the farthest?

The Arctic Tern. Each year it journeys over 27,000 miles. That is like flying around the whole planet!

What's the largest fish?

The Whale Shark. It can grow to be 65 feet long. That's about as long as 5 mini-vans!